TRAVELS WITH AN OLD GUITAR

TRAVELS WITH AN OLD GUITAR

A TALE OF MY WANDERING

JIM BROWN

This is dedicated to my marvellous children Joe and Jenny for whom I started this project

* * *

1.

To Tony
All THE BEST

Jim Brown

TABLE OF CONTENTS

PART 1

1 - BEGINNING 1

2 - BRIGHTON 8

3 - SOUTHAMPTON 17

4 - ATLANTIC...25

5 - CANADA 36

6 - CALGARY...46

7 - ALBERTA..53

8 - STAMPEDE 60

9 - THE BAND..72

10 - GAYLE 84

11 - PARTING...96

PART 2

12 - VANCOUVER 105

13 - PENTICTON..114

14 - RETURN TO CALGARY 127

i

15 - PENTICTON II 136

15 - PINE STREET 147

16 - CALIFORNIA 155

17 - MEXICO 164

18 - HOUSEBOAT 176

19 - CALIFORNIA HITCHHIKING 185

20 - DRIFTING 193

PART 3

21 - SUE 198

22 - JOE 204

23 - FRANCE - JENNY 213

24 - ENGLAND 224

25 - JUNE - NEW ZEALAND 232

26 - CONCLUSIONS 250

27 - MOMENTS IN PARADISE 261

28 - LYMINGTON 274

FOREWORD

It started with a footprint on the ceiling, dear reader. It was a mystery how it got there and I got blamed for it by his father, but I know it was Jim Brown who put it there.

We were having a band practice in his flat and I'm sure it was his way of telling us in the early days of our group 'The Zodiacs', when we were mere lads, that he was going to travel - and so he did as you will see from this highly readable narrative of his world travels.

Jim is a wandering troubadour who has brought pleasure to many with his music, and since the 60s I have been honoured to call him a close friend. I know you will enjoy his life story.

It all started with our band and the great music we made in those days. Those were times I know that neither of us will ever forget.

So I hope you enjoy reading about his adventures and you agree with me that Jim has led a very interesting life.

Sir Peter Field

PREFACE

My wandering began in the springtime of 1964. I wanted to see some of those exotic-sounding far-away places I had heard about and see them for myself. I was off on the grand adventure, just me and my old guitar, the only constant thing in my life throughout those times, and together we were to have many interesting experiences.

What follows is a description of my journey across the world, the unexpected adventures that ensued, the impressions made upon me and how my life changed over the years. I have tried to describe my innermost thoughts on that long journey of discovery and how I perceived it all as it happened. It was a great journey of discovery for me.

I lived the life of a nomad in the early days, just drifting, and to steal a line from Dylan:- 'with no direction home'. Hitchhiking with the open road ahead was my greatest pleasure. I was unencumbered and my spirit rode high. Those were the times when I could feel a sense of total freedom.

I needed to grow a few roots between times but the horizon was ever in my sight.

Music has always been my great love and I was fortunate to play in bands in England, Canada and New Zealand.

I don't regret one moment and would happily do it all again. I had some marvellous times.

I believe that we all have a story that's worth telling, I know I certainly do, for if they aren't told, they are lost forever when we depart this world, blown away like fallen leaves.

So here is mine.

PART 1

1

BEGINNING

As I leaned on the rail of the ship looking out to sea with the seagulls screaming overhead, I was filled with excitement. 1964 was that time when the madness of 'Beatlemania' was everywhere. Swinging London was where it was all happening and England was the main attraction. But I was leaving it all for pastures new. Swinging London, the green hills of the Sussex Downs, the streets of my hometown of Brighton, and all of those things familiar to me would soon be left far behind.

It is more than fifty years now since I began that journey, and over such a vast period the memory begins to fade a little. It seems like a lifetime ago, but I remember much of what happened clearly, as it was the most exciting and adventurous part of my life. I was cutting out on my own and looking for adventure. It was a time of introspection for me too, with thoughts of the past as well as the future as I gazed out over the water. I had thoughts of sadness at the recent partings from my family and friends, but also great excitement about all that might lie before me. I had a head full of dreams and I wanted to travel. Nothing less would satisfy my wandering spirit.

The cinema had given me tantalising glimpses of exotic places, like Tahiti and Hawaii, with warm sunny beaches populated by beautiful girls. Well, that was the dream they had sold us, and I wanted some of it. There was not much chance of me being surrounded by those lovely hula girls in Canada. It was more likely that I would encounter snow, ice, and bears, but it was just the beginning. I had found the opportunity to travel and that was good enough for me.

The Franconia

I was realising my dream and it felt wonderful. For the first time in my life, I felt free. I had discarded all of my ties and was unencumbered by the constraints of ordinary life. That

Beginning

sense of leaving everything behind, shaking it all off, and for that moment, not belonging anywhere, with the excitement of moving on towards the unknown, were feelings I was moved to seek many times again, often abandoning a perfectly good life for uncertainty. But they were the times which gave me the greatest happiness and lifted my spirit to pure joy.

I had no good reason to be leaving England other than those feelings. I had a loving family and a full social life with many friends. I had a job working in a lawyer's office with prospects to advance in the legal profession and I was playing guitar in a band. So why would I leave? After all, England in the 1960s was *the* place to be. It had emerged from the dark ages after the war, and it belonged to the young, to my generation. It was a time of great optimism for us when we would not follow our parents' way of doing things but would reshape the world and do things our way. 'The times they were a-changin', as Bob Dylan would soon remind us. Maybe every generation of youth feels something of this when they reach maturity, but my generation of the 1950s and 1960s certainly did. There was an atmosphere of positive change in the air and we felt we were living in a new era of enlightenment where all things were possible.

My job in the Lawyer's office amounted to little more than being an office boy. It was all rather mundane boring work. I was sixteen years old when I started to work there for the huge sum of three pounds and ten shillings a week. Not a vast sum of money even then. My new boss enthusiastically given me a pile of law books to read as he was keen for me to get serious about the legal profession. It was a great opportunity for me I suppose, but I couldn't seem to find the enthusiasm for it at all. For one thing, I had just started playing bass guitar with the band and my head was still in Tahiti with those lovely hula girls. Well, I *was* just sixteen.

My desire to travel started in my schooldays when I pored over my atlas and wondered about those faraway places with exotic-sounding names. They were just names on a map, but they fascinated me and I wanted to see them for myself. The prospect of staying put and making my way up through the legal profession filled me with horror. I had to find some means of escape.

So, this is the story of the times I had in the ensuing years after deciding that I would go to live in Canada, leaving England behind me, and as I trawl through my memories, I want to put down some of those things that happened to me way back then, and what it was like for that youthful me of so long ago. There were some amazingly good times up ahead and of course some sad disappointments too.

There is so much to remember. I did not appreciate then how far-reaching my decision to set off on that first journey would turn out to be, for me and my family, and others. We sometimes make small decisions in life that turn out to have large consequences.

It was a bright sunny day in early May when it all began for me. My Dad, my brother Paul, and I loaded up Dad's Volkswagen Beetle with my cases at my home in Sussex and from there they drove me to Southampton where I was to join the ship with a suitcase and a large cabin trunk containing all of my worldly possessions. There was no limit in those days to the amount of luggage that you could take on such a journey by sea. I had stuff in there that I would never use. My mum had provided me with an iron, which I don't believe I ever used, and I had more clothes and junk in there than I would ever need. Some objects must have meant something to me at the time. I remember a toreador's hat, some badges, books, and many other things that I can't remember. Why I thought I would need those things I don't know. They were of no practical use and have long since vanished from my world along with the trunk.

I was the youngest, and the last of three brothers to leave those shores. My oldest brother, Ronn, was in Singapore with the Royal Air Force and my other brother, Paul, had just returned from a stint in Cyprus, also with The Royal Air Force, and now Dad was taking son number three to flee Britain.

My ship was named 'The Franconia' on the Cunard Line, destined for Montreal in Quebec, but this was just the first stage of my journey as I was ultimately heading further west to Calgary in Alberta.

It was springtime, the time of new beginnings, new growth, and the blooming of nature, and it was the time for a new beginning for me too. I was quite inexperienced in life, and not at all ready to tackle all that I would encounter, with no thoughts of danger or of what might become of me. I was just filled with youthful optimism, excitement and exhilaration. It was the beginning of the great adventure as I watched England disappear into the mist behind me beyond the foam from the ship's stern.

Travels with an old guitar

Farewell to England

Once we were fully underway I stood on the deck of the ship gazing out on the vastness of the great Atlantic Ocean and was amazed at the view. In every direction just an endless sea, as far as the distant horizon. The immensity of it was staggering. Our ship was an island, disconnected from everything but the great ocean. It brought a real sense of isolation from the rest of humanity.

I thought about what had led me to be there. I had made the decision to go on this journey without any idea as to whether it was sensible or stupid, but the decision was made and it would turn out to be a pivotal turning point in my life. I had fond memories of the many things that I was leaving behind, like Mum's cooking; homemade doughnuts, and other such delights, and her constant love and support. I had fond memories of my dad too and how much closer we had become over the past few months since I had gone to live with him, and the good times, fun, and laughter we had shared.

I would miss my friends too as I remembered their words of affection, and how they would miss me when I left them for the last time. But despite this sadness at all that I was leaving behind, my spirit was riding at the top of a wave as I entered this new phase of my life. The feeling was intoxicating.

* * *

2

BRIGHTON

Before embarking on the story of my journey and my time in Canada and beyond, I should take a little diversion and begin by describing a little more about my early background.

I was born in Brighton, Sussex-by-the-sea, and lived there until the age of eighteen, so I had no experience of any other place in this world. But I had been fortunate in living there, as it was a great place to grow up. Brighton is a place where you can be free to be yourself whatever that might be, without having to conform to any kind of 'normal'. Anything goes in Brighton, and the open-minded freedom that prevails there was perfectly conducive to my spirit. There was also the ever-present sea which never ceased to fascinate me. I was an introspective boy, and would often walk the seashore to let my imagination wander. I was drawn to it to watch the endless movement of the waves and wonder about what lay beyond the horizon. I loved the sea. It connected me to those places that intrigued me and I never tired of watching it in all seasons.

We three brothers must have had a nomadic gene as my two older siblings, Ronn, (he spells it this way), and Paul, had already left home and travelled far across the world by the time I reached those confusing adolescent years, so my desire to wander the world was perhaps inevitable.

My oldest brother Ronn, was adopted into our family when he was ten and I was five. His earlier life had been very troubled as he had no parent able to look after him, so to our great fortune, he came into our family. He became my brother and was as much a part as if he were born into it. Ronn became a first-class older brother and always looked after me in many ways. When he joined the Royal Air Force and was earning money for the first time, he would treat me to things that would otherwise be beyond my reach, like a new made-to-measure Italian suit and my first, rather unsuccessful contact lenses. My other brother, Paul, was three years older than me and was already there. He subsequently joined me in some of my adventures in Canada, so there is more about him later.

My Mum and Dad had separated when I was about ten, although any recollection of their separation is lost to my memory. But it had been an amicable parting, and they remained in close contact for the rest of their lives. My brothers and I lived with Mum but we would see Dad when he came to see us or take us out, and at those times we would experience a very different world from our own.

Their lifestyles were words apart. Mum liked the simple life. She was a strong-willed independent person and would try her hand at many things. She had a great 'can do' attitude. It was a struggle for her financially to bring up three boys on her own, but we managed.

Dad, on the other hand, was busy climbing the social ladder and had great ambitions for a better style of living. He was moving in higher circles. Both of our parents had come from very poor beginnings, but their take on life grew differently. However, as a result, to our good fortune, we boys benefitted by experiencing two contrasting ways of living and learned to fit into either social situation with ease. We became chameleons.

Dad had been brought up in a very religious family and that influenced the way that we were brought up, so my brothers and I grew up quite conversant with the Baptist church. We had to go there three times every Sunday and I can remember sneaking down the road every Sunday morning in my best duds, with my bible well hidden under my coat, trying not to catch the eye of my pals playing football on the green. 'Lucky them', I thought, but I had no choice in the matter.

Our home with Mum was a happy place and my brothers and I had a wonderful time, growing up with complete freedom. We were able to go on small adventures of our own and to wander wherever we pleased around Sussex. Train fares were cheap and we had bikes. We were fortunate to have such a mum to give us the love and freedom to grow. It gave all of us a great foundation for life.

We made soapbox carts and learned the skill of making working bows and arrows using yew branches from the forest just outside Brighton. We made up bikes from bits and pieces of other deceased bikes, all in the entrance hallway to our basement flat. We were forever making things and learned how to be very creative in figuring out how things worked with very few resources. We lived on the edge of a green where there were trees to climb and lots of other boys to play football with. Mum's main objective in life was for us to be happy and fed. Food, for Mum, was ever important.

There were always plenty of boys at our house as Mum would readily take in our friends, often to stay with us for several days, such as when we all came down with the flu.

Girls though were another thing altogether. There were no girls. I had two brothers, no sisters, and I had been to a boys' school, so girls were a strange mystery to me altogether. They were an unknown species. They certainly interested me when I reached adolescence. My hormones told me that they were just what I needed, but they were quite beyond my knowledge. I didn't know the first thing about them and the truth is they scared me a little. Their mystery and allure held real power. I had much to learn. My adventurous discovery of girls was far off yet.

I was quite inhibited, self-conscious, and full of self-doubt as a young boy. I was goofy with protruding teeth until I had a lot of dental work done, and I wore glasses that were getting thicker and thicker every time I visited the optician. That all left its mark on me. So there I lived happily with Mum until I left school at sixteen when a new horizon appeared.

Dad invited me to go and live with him in his house in Shoreham, just along the coast from Brighton. It was a great plan as I had not had the chance to get to know him well as we had only ever seen him on flying visits. So I moved in with him, and this was the beginning of two years of great times for both of us. He was very young in spirit and full of fun. I enjoyed living with him very much.

Travels with an old guitar

He bought me a Lambretta scooter which gave me mobility to get back to Brighton to see my friends. That was the era of the Mods and Rockers and having a scooter put me firmly in the category of 'Mod', but to me, the scooter was just a means of transport. It suited my needs at the time perfectly.

Jim being strangled.

I should introduce the guitar to my story at this time. It has played a big part in my life and was a link to many of the things that happened to me over the years. It has opened doors for me to social life, and it even played a part in my meeting a certain young lady who was to become a very important part of my life, which I will describe later. I was never a virtuoso guitar player but have spent a lifetime playing and singing and have enjoyed being able to entertain people here and there over the years.

My old Jazz Radiotone guitar

Rock music and Rhythm and Blues had arrived. It was *our* music, the music, of the young, and it was great to be a part of that movement.

My first band when I was around sixteen went under the name of Pete and the Zodiacs. In those early days, we played tunes by The Shadows, inspired by the magical sounds of Hank Marvin's guitar, and songs by Cliff Richard and other pop stars. But then along came The Beatles who turned the world insane, so we started doing their songs, and those by The Rolling Stones, The Animals, and others. We were just one band among many in Brighton, playing in pubs and at dances. I have long since lost touch with the other guys, except for my good friend Pete, who was our singer.

My life has periodically been that of a nomad, as you will see from this tale of mine, but Pete has always been a stable, upstanding character. He has done much over the years to help the homeless and those less fortunate people in our society. Until recently, he was Lord-Lieutenant of East Sussex, the Queen's representative, or "Lord Lefty" as some of us call him, and at the time of this writing he has just been knighted as Sir Peter, but to me, Pete, he remains, the same old buddy, always ready to have fun or a joke. He remains a true friend who I value deeply. We have known each other since we were sixteen, and now we are in our seventies.

'Pete and the Zodiacs':- Alan Brown (no relation) - Jim
Dave - Phil -- Back row -- Pete - John.

Brighton

So that little diversion from my main story was my background before I went a-travelling. I had a wealth of good memories of all of these things that happened around me as a boy growing up in Brighton, but I was leaving it all behind as I set off on my journey.

The reason that Canada was to be my destination was that in my quest to travel and explore this great big world, Dad had suggested that we write to his sister, Grace, who lived in Calgary, Alberta, to see whether I could go there. So after a short to-and-fro by letter, she said that I would be welcome to go to live with her and her family. She had two sons of a similar age to me, two cousins I had never met. Ron was a year older than me and Doug, was two years younger. Sadly, within a few years, great tragedy lay ahead for cousin Ron which I will describe later.

All I knew of Calgary was that it was a cowboy town, and home of the biggest rodeo in North America, The Calgary Stampede.

I had an open door, at last, to set off to explore the world. There were no obstacles in my way. I had made up my mind I would go off to the land of bears and ice, the Rocky Mountains, Cowboys, and Indians. It was an exciting prospect, but it would mean leaving behind my whole world, and all I had ever known. It would also mean leaving my mum behind. I wondered how she would feel. Would she raise objections and not want me to go? But when it came to it, I found this was way off the mark. Mum also had a wandering spirit and wished she could go too, so she gave me her warm approval. Of course, she would miss me but I think she understood my feelings very well. It was great to have her approval and wishes of happiness for me. I would carry her with me. But still in the end, when the time came to say goodbye to her, and I set off on my Lambretta, I had to stop many times on the roadside. My tears were blinding me.

3

SOUTHAMPTON

My dad must have been accustomed to seeing his sons depart from England by then. He was a true Englishman who thought that the only sensible thing to be was English. All other countries were poor imitations of civilised culture. I had dabbled with the idea of going to Australia but he had said no to that,

"Don't go there Jim, they are all convicts" He was always full of jokes. He didn't object to my going to Canada though as his sister lived there, and he felt that he was able to be comfortable about my going there. He knew I would be alright there, but for him, England was the land he loved.

Dad was also starting on a new journey of his own when I was leaving as he had re-married just two weeks before my departure. He and Winnie had known each other for a long time and they had decided to marry, So the time of my departure marked the end of an era for both of us and a new start. Life always changes.

Those two years living with Dad had been marvellous. We were always having friends around at the house for a meal or to listen to music. He was a great fan of the classics and although I was more interested in the music of my era, "R and B" and pop at the time, through him I did get a wider view of music and enjoyed listening to his records.

He introduced me to the music from his youth, the wartime era of the 1940s with records of Fats Waller, one of our favourites, Louis Armstrong and Charles Trenet, among many others that we would listen to while he burned the sausages. We both liked burnt sausages. I also liked the sound and atmosphere of the big band era by Glenn Miller and such bands which we played as the kitchen filled with smoke. Our home was always filled with an interesting mix of sounds from the record player and smoke.

Dad even took an interest in the popular songs of my era. He would sometimes come along with Winnie to the pubs where I was playing with my band, and some of those were very dodgy places indeed. I have such fond memories of my dad with his great sense of humour and fun and his wonderful story-telling, often entertaining a small gathering in a pub with his rambling tales. I will always treasure those days we spent together.

But my journey was beginning. There we were at Southampton docks, surrounded by great ocean-going liners destined for all parts of the world. As the three of us, Paul, Dad, and I looked up from the dockside at my ship it seemed enormous. I couldn't imagine how a ship so vast could be much affected by the sea, but how wrong I was. I had no real concept of how powerful the oceans were. In the mid-ocean, even a large ship could be tossed around by gigantic waves. I also didn't know then how fortunate I was to be experiencing a wonderful method of travel that would soon be gone forever to the competition from cheap air flights. Those great days of affordable voyages on the wonderful ocean liners were coming to an end, but I had no thoughts of those things then. I was there simply to enjoy it to the full. I had a whole new life ahead of me.

I was about to board the ship, heading off into the unknown to make a new start in Canada. I was, to put it mildly, excited. I had all of those memories of England in the back of my mind as I looked up from the dockside at the mighty ship and not for the first time my stomach felt a little uneasy. Dad looked at me with concern.

"Don't worry Jim, you'll be OK," he reassured me.

The ship would take me across the Atlantic Ocean, a voyage of about a week, and then, after cruising down the recently thawed St. Lawrence River, would dock in Montreal, Quebec, where I would disembark. From there I would take the train to Toronto, Ontario, and after a brief stopover to visit a family friend, I would continue westward to Calgary by rail travelling across the prairies of central Canada. This journey would take three or four more days. The whole trip would take me about eleven days in all, plus however many days I spent in Toronto.

Travels with an old guitar

As the time for our departure approached there was much activity on the ship and the dockside, with people coming and going, trying to find their way around, while freight and luggage were being loaded by crane. I looked at the faces all around me and wondered just who were my fellow adventurers. Who among them would I get to know? Who among them was sending their loved ones away to pastures new? There was a great buzz of excitement in the air.

Dad and Paul had come on board with me and the ship was a maze, but after a brief search, we found our way down to my cabin, my new temporary home, which was deep down on one of the lower decks, somewhere underwater if the truth were known. I had a sink, a bed, and not much else, but it was all that I needed to get started on my life of wandering. I had my old bashed-up guitar, my constant companion with which I might expose my soul from time to time. Life really would be lonesome without that comfortable old friend.

Dad, Paul, Jim

So the three of us sat celebrating with a beer talking about family, travels past and future, and many other things while we had a last chance to share a drink. It might be the last that we would share for a long time. A journey to the other side of the world often meant a long separation, maybe for years. None of us knew how long it would be.

Travels with an old guitar

It was a very significant moment in my life as I sat there with my dad and my brother. It would just be me from then on, having to look out for myself. I would have to deal with everything that came to me without help. Would I be able to cope? So we savoured those last moments together, each with his thoughts. At moments like those, the family becomes very important. This scene must have been played out many times in many places over the years, but at least my prospects were not as bleak as they might have been in historical times when people would have known that this was the end with no possibility of return.

Then, all too soon it seemed, and probably before we were quite ready for it, the loudspeaker system announced that all visitors should leave the ship. So came yet another time of goodbyes. This was the last of many that I had had to go through over the past few weeks. I'd had to say farewell to my friends, the guys in the band, work colleagues, Mum, and now to my dad and brother. They were all difficult partings and I have never been good at goodbyes. My emotions were never far below the surface. So we made our sad farewells with hugs and promises to keep in touch. Dad and Paul set off making for the gangway, while I made my way up onto the open deck to try to spot them on the dockside.

I was feeling very emotional with a lump in my throat and a tear in my eye as I faced this final farewell. I had no idea if or when I might return to England. My life was about to become very different from that moment on and I knew it.

I felt quite alone as I stood there on the deck, although

people were all around me. There we all were heading off to who knows what and where, all of my fellow passengers and little old me, a very green, inexperienced traveller.

There was so much happening all around me in those final moments on the ship and the dockside in preparation for our departure, as people made their final farewells. Eventually, all was clear, the walkway was removed, and the heavy ropes securing us to the dock were taken away, the ship's horn blew loudly two or three times and very slowly, imperceptibly at first, the ship started to move. Goodness knows where this would lead me. But how exhilarated I felt. I could see Dad and Paul in the crowd, waving, as the ship slipped away, while alongside me, all along the ship's rail we waved and shouted one last time. Many tears were shed that day as we slowly lost sight of our loved ones and families.

Jim

Travels with an old guitar

It was all up to me now. I was flying with no safety net.

* * *

4

ATLANTIC

My journey had begun. After leaving the waters around Southampton, I had all the time in the world to just relax and enjoy it.

The ship first headed to Le Havre in France and then on to Southern Ireland to gather a few more hopeful wanderers before embarking on the great Atlantic Ocean.

It was such a pleasure to travel in an unhurried way and

to make a holiday of it, quite unlike the rush and stress involved with flying.

The voyage on the ship was a luxury holiday in itself, even for somebody travelling on an emigrant fare as I was. The food, the service, and all that were provided for us on board were of very high quality. There were amusements and amenities of all kinds, including a cinema, shops, bars, and live entertainment by a band in the dance hall every evening. We had three wonderful full-course meals a day in the dining room with as much free wine as we wanted, a swimming pool, deck games and more. The only ongoing expense was for drinks from the bars, but these were very cheap.

The first thing for me to do was explore the ship in more detail and wander through the various decks to find out where everything was.

On the uppermost open deck, were the swimming pool and games facilities, deck chairs, and umbrellas in case the sun should shine down upon us, and here I also found the spacious lounge and ballroom. The bars there were open at any hour. making it all too easy to fall victim to for a young, foolish man.

As I moved on down through the lower decks I found the huge dining room, which was set up with approximately a million tables, each accommodating ten people. There were shops, a cinema, a hairdresser, a sports area, and the purser's office where strange foreign money could be purchased, and the storage of valuables could be arranged, of which I had none. Moving on down I came to the passengers' cabins on the lower decks. I could see I was in for a great time. All I needed then to make my journey more comfortable was to retrieve my suitcase. Good luck with that Jim.

The onboard luggage was being delivered to an open space beside the purser's office, so I made my way there. And there I waited, jostling with the other passengers while I watched them come and go with their suitcases, and still, I waited until I stood alone. My suitcase never arrived. A few days later, Dad opened up the trunk of his car and to his horror, there was my case with all my necessary goods for a comfortable journey. I just had the clothes that I stood in, my old guitar, and nothing more. It was not a very good start. It looked as if my first attempt at being independent had failed miserably. It was a good thing that there was a shop on board where I could replenish a few items to keep me going, and once it was clear that my suitcase and I were not going to be reunited, that's just what I did. I had a large trunk in the hold of the ship, unavailable to me, full of stuff that would ultimately turn out to be of little or no use anyway, which travelled on to the end of my journey in Calgary.

After a day or two at sea, I made some friends around my age, and we would often sit on the open deck with my guitar, singing songs together. It was interesting to compare notes with them as to what had brought us together. Some were travelling to pastures new with their parents, but I wasn't the only lone, young traveller. There were other explorers there too. Those would be brief acquaintances, but we shared just a short moment in our lives, and at the end of the journey we parted never to see each other again. I have sometimes wondered how they fared, and where they ended up. I wonder if any of them ever wrote of those times or related any of it to their children.

The cinema ran films of all kinds, including some of the latest movies, but there were also some interesting short ones about Canada, its culture, and the people, the cities, the native people, their customs and way of life, and all of these gave us a glimpse into the way that some Canadians lived. To us aliens, they were a good introduction to the land that was to be our new home. They showed aspects of Canadian life that were very different and a world away culturally from the life that I knew.

As our journey got underway, the first real point of social contact was at the restaurant table, where my little group had been thrown together for the week. The food was excellent, with wine in constant supply as the waiters rushed around trying to keep their charges happy and well-supplied with all they wanted.

The dining style was rather highbrow with the tables laid out with fine cutlery, strange forks and far too many knives. It all looked quite luxurious to my eyes. The older people seemed to make a point of being properly dressed for dinner. I was from a simple background and it all seemed rather posh to me. However, I had already learned how to do 'posh' back in England as Dad would sometimes take me as a guest to classy dinner functions which he attended in connection with his profession as am estate agent and member of the valuers institute This was in stark contrast to my simple life at home, but I found it an easy game to play. Remember, I was a chameleon.

As the days went on, we fellow diners introduced

ourselves, and each told our story of how we came to be there. Naturally, we were a mixed group in age and background; some older people, one newly married couple, and a few younger single delayed pioneers like me. I was the youngest in our company and was probably the least worldly-wise in the group. Some had already travelled the world and revelled in the telling of tales of places where they had been, while I had little to tell and was just beginning the grand adventure. Some, like me, were off to start a new life in Canada, but I remember one man who confessed that his only reason for being there was that he saw this route to Canada simply as an easy stepping stone to what he wanted, which was an entry to the USA. Others of the group were travelling to visit relatives and some were just on holiday. So the conversations that we had around the dinner table allowed everyone to become a storyteller, which also revealed character.

I had seen movies of ships' voyages, many of them revolving around shipboard romances. Oh, I should be so lucky! But alas my ignorance of women remained complete for a while yet. But not forever.

At the start of the voyage, the large dining room was full of people, but as time went on and the sea got rougher in the mid-Atlantic our company got thinner each day with many half-empty tables. There came a time when I wasn't there either.

In the evenings, listening to the band in the lounge, and indulging in the amazingly cheap booze, drinking with my new friends became very relaxing. I was becoming very chilled out. Well, ok, I was becoming very drunk, often staggering back to my cabin in very poor condition. The clocks would change by one hour each day, which made it very easy to adjust to the changing time zones, with no such thing as jet lag.

I had become friendly with a middle-aged English couple, a man and his wife, who were seated at the same dining table as me. They were going to Ontario, to join their son, as immigrants to Canada like me, and I think that they felt that I needed looking-after. This was all a long time ago now and I cannot remember their names so I will call them Mr and Mrs Ontario.

So one day, as I was walking on the deck, I saw Mr Ontario hurrying towards me. He had been looking for me all over the ship as he had managed to get an invitation for a guided tour of the engine room for two, and he wanted me to go along with him. It was a lucky break that most passengers didn't get.

I followed him to a meeting place where we linked up with a few others and a guide, and from there we were escorted into some of the deepest parts of the ship to see the mechanics that kept us moving.

We went down and down until we must have been deep underwater and could go no lower. Below us, just beyond the floor that we stood on, was the cold green sea. It was deafeningly noisy down there, and the guide had to shout to be heard. What we saw was a colossal engine that was driving two propeller shafts that disappeared through the back of the ship. Everything there was on a vast scale. The immense size of the propeller shafts is what is lodged in my memory. The propellers themselves just beyond us in the sea must have been equally huge. This place was of course at the back of the ship which I realise is a highly un-nautical term. If I was a sailor I would probably have said the stern, but what do I know? Anyway, we were at the back of the ship down at the bottom. I had been very fortunate to see all of this with Mr Ontario and was glad to have had the chance. It was masterful engineering on a vast scale.

After several days at sea, I was sitting at our dining table when I noticed that one of the waiters serving a nearby table looked familiar. I watched him for a while and became convinced I knew him, so eventually, I just had to find out and went to speak with him. I was right. He was a cousin of my very good Scottish friend Tony, back in Brighton, and I had met him a year or two earlier when he was visiting there. His name was Ian and he hailed from Glasgow. It was Ian with the incomprehensible Scottish accent. He remembered me, and after we had chatted for a while, he invited me to come to meet him in the crew's quarters when he was off duty later that day. At least I think that's what he said. Ian had joined the merchant navy and was working for the Cunard Line, travelling back and forth across the Atlantic.

So sometime later I made my way to meet him, whereupon he led me through a doorway leading to the crew's part of the ship, which would normally be out of bounds for the passengers. It was immediately noticeable that this was a very different environment from the rest of the ship in that everything seemed to be stark and functional with very narrow corridors, exposed pipes everywhere, no attempt at the decor, and even more basic cabin accommodation than mine. Ian guided me through a maze of corridors until we came to a very small cabin that was crowded with off-duty crew: a mixed bag of people from many places, with all sorts of accents, some even stranger than Ian's, each telling their tall tales, real or imagined. They were trying to outdo each other with wilder and wilder stories of things they had supposedly done. One-up-manship prevailed.

As soon as we arrived, I was handed a large glass of rum which I was expected and encouraged to drink down in one go, just like the rest of them. It was a very macho environment, and I guess they were putting me through some sort of initiation process. This glass was followed by another and another and so it went on until within a short time I was barely able to talk, stand, or function at all. I really should have known better, but there we are, I was only eighteen years old and still had much to learn. I had had no previous experience with rum, and after this would not be in a hurry to try it again. Sometime later I could be found wandering through a warren of corridors, quite lost and quite drunk, weaving my way back to eventually find my cabin where I fell on my bed and passed out. I somehow survived this incident but the experience left its mark on me and to this day, I cannot face even a hint of rum.

We made headway across the great Atlantic Ocean and as the days went on we amused ourselves with games, music, conversation, and movies, while I learned a few lessons about alcohol. It was marvellous. I was still relishing my freedom and life felt very good indeed. I spent many hours leaning on the ship's rail gazing around at the huge emptiness of the ocean, thinking of my past and future. I had no worries at all and was a very happy man. It felt marvellous.

One day I received a message to go to the ship's radio communications room to receive a phone call from my brother, Paul, which was a pleasant surprise.

We were well into our journey, and not far from Canada, when the word went out that icebergs had been seen nearby, so I made my way to the upper deck to see for myself. They were some distance away but still looked huge. The obvious thought to me then, and no doubt to many others was of the "Titanic" which went down to the cold depths, taking all those poor souls with it in 1912, in a place that was not many miles from where we were.

On another occasion, we saw a group of whales that had been spotted near the ship. This journey certainly opened my eyes to some new sights.

I was learning to have great respect for the power of the sea. In the mid-Atlantic, the waves were huge and although the ship was enormous, it was thrown around at times as the weather deteriorated. This had its effect on many of us and I was often incapacitated on more than one count. Seasickness, from the constant rolling of the deck, was one, and booze was another. Sometimes it was a combination of the two. I had moved on from rum to gin, but this was equally lethal to me. I didn't seem to be cut out for those heavy spirits. I should stick to beer. The place where these effects could be most easily dealt with was on the open deck, where one could at least watch and anticipate the sway of the ship and where if an ejection was imminent and unavoidable the ship's rail was the best place to be. After being on board for a few days, we adjusted to walking with a rolling motion to counteract the ever-present swaying of the ship, and when we eventually set foot on dry land again the lack of motion felt very odd and took a little while for reorientation.

We had been at sea for a week when in due course, we approached the finale of our journey.

"Land ho!" was the traditional call that I had seen in the old movies of sea voyages, pirates, explorers and such, and one day, although these were almost certainly not the actual words used, land was indeed 'ho'. So the word went out, and after a full week of being an island universe, surrounded by nothing but water as far as could be seen, we turned out onto the upper deck to view the scene.

Canada! There it was! So this, at last, was the land I had been reading about. The land of cowboys, mountains, Indians, and all the rest. I cautiously crept upstairs, or above as opposed to below, or whatever the nautical term might be for the open upper deck, to see for myself. I say 'cautiously' because I was hungover, sick, with my head spinning. Foolish boy! But, despite my fragile condition, this was a sight not to be missed.

There it was, Newfoundland. What an inspired imaginative name! It was my first view of Canada, and I was huddled up in a blanket, sick, weary, and very, very fragile.

Atlantic

The immigration authorities came out to the ship to process us before we were permitted to land. It was such an easy thing then. As long as you were fit and healthy and ready to work, you were welcome. I wish that today's youth could so easily fulfil their dreams and travel as freely as I did. For me, it was all very straightforward, and after answering a few questions from the Canadian immigration officer, my passport was stamped allowing me to enter the country.

We then had a further full day's travel on the ship as we cruised down the St Lawrence River through Nova Scotia and Quebec towards Montreal, and for me, this was a little more welcomed recovery time from my fragile condition. I would need to learn to look after myself more carefully. It was a very pleasant and smooth last lap, giving me my first view of a Canadian landscape, with low, rolling hills and brightly painted houses on the riverside, quite unlike crowded English houses and towns. I found it intriguing and I wondered about the people who lived there. What were they like? How did they live? How different were they from the English? How would they respond to me? I found this to be a very pleasant, contemplative interlude.

It was time to disembark and feel the ground beneath my feet once again. Time to set foot in my new homeland, and find out what it was really like. I had arrived.

* * *

5

CANADA

So this was Canada. How did it feel? What was it like? My first impression was that it looked much like the America that I had seen on the big screen. The people seemed to speak the same to my untrained ear. I recognised it at once. It was USA North, just like in the movies. The first leg of my journey, the transatlantic crossing, was over. I had been on the ship for a week since leaving Southampton, and we had arrived at Montreal in French Quebec, where, after stepping off the ship I was able to plant my feet on the solid unmoving ground again that didn't pitch and roll. My school French was rather sparse so I hoped I wouldn't be accosted in that language or I would be lost.

I made my way to the railway station where I was to board a train for the next leg of my journey to Toronto, which was to be the first stage of my trip out to the far West. I was fascinated as I made my way into the station, taking in all the sights and sounds that were a mixture of both familiar and strange. My senses were heightened and tuned in to all of the differences that I saw and heard around me. My journey to the station was very nearly terminated by my stepping out into the road and looking the wrong way. These fools drove on the wrong side of the road. It was a close call, but I was still intact and found the station without difficulty, where I set about searching for the right train to take me to Toronto. I was to have a short stay there with Colin, a friend of the family, before heading out to Calgary.

But first I needed some food. I was getting hungry and my nose led me to a hot dog kiosk in the middle of the busy concourse. Now came my first real experience of being an alien. The man asked me what I wanted and I replied,

"Hot dog, please." His reply was incomprehensible to me. What he said was "Mustardnrelish?"

I had no idea what he was talking about. I recognised the word mustard, that was clear enough. It was the "nrelish" that threw me. My sheltered life had never exposed me to what sounded like 'relish'. What the hell was relish? And is that what he actually said? I replied, "Pardon?"

He looked at me with some annoyance and repeated, "Mustardnrelish?" The second time was no clearer to me than the first. I still wasn't sure where I was going with this. I was still just as confused.

"Pardon?" By now people were starting to turn around and look at me as if I were simple. The man behind the counter was looking exasperated, so I took the safe way out and just said "OK" not knowing what I would get while trying my best to look sane. I gave him a handful of coins that meant nothing to me, and what he gave me in return was something that vaguely resembled a hot dog. However, I'd never encountered a sausage quite like that before, and this was covered with sickly sweet mustard and a green substance. I guess this was the 'nrelish'. It also contained a strange pickled object which seemed to have no business having such an intimate relationship with a hot dog. This I extracted and ejected into a nearby bin. I was hungry, so I ate the strange hot dog anyway and wondered what other gems like this awaited me in this land. And so I made my way to the train for Toronto with the realisation that I would have to learn a new language.

I boarded my train and settled in for the long ride of just over three hundred miles, partially fed on that strange hot dog, but there was plenty more food available on the train. My initial impressions were that everything I had seen so far seemed to be on a much larger scale than in England. The cars, the buildings, the roads, and the meals, almost everything seemed to be bigger. As I travelled westward across the prairies, even the sky looked bigger and seemed to expand to huge proportions to fit the wide-open land. The train, just like everything else, was huge compared with the trains back home. The journey to Toronto was an overnighter, and when I arrived, there waiting to pick me up was our friend Colin, the first familiar face I had seen since leaving England a week before.

Colin was a couple of years older than me and had worked with Dad in his estate agents' business. He had moved out to Toronto from England the year before. I had met him several times in the past, and he had kindly offered to put me up in his apartment for a while before I journeyed on to my destination in the West. He, like me, was out to experience new adventures in a land far from home. We drove to his apartment, which was on a high rise in the heart of town. I had seen high-rise buildings before, but Toronto had more than its fair share. There were hundreds of them, but that was the norm there. It was fairly typical of North American cities, giving them their characteristic appearance, but it was all new to me.

My stay with Colin gave me a good introduction to Canada and he had recently been through similar experiences to those that I would be encountering. He explained some of the cultural differences I was likely to come across, along with some of the language pitfalls that I might fall into. I would discover plenty of those for myself, but he gave me an alien's survival lesson. He was very hospitable, feeding me steaks every night and looking out for my welfare.

One day, he took me on a trip to Niagara Falls, not far from Toronto. Niagara straddles the border of Canada and the U.S.A. and so it was there, just across the water that I had my first view of that country. As children, we had been raised on everything American from the movies, so it was a thrill for me to lay eyes on the place for real for the first time.

We went on a conducted tour, which took us beneath the falls, dressed in large coverall waterproofs, down through passages, until we came to a cave where you could look out through the rushing water. It was quite amazing to be viewing that immense curtain of water right in front of us and one got the sense of the power of the falls. We got wet. The guide told us of a legend, how in ancient times the local Iroquois Indians would send a young maiden over the falls in a canoe, as a sacrifice presumably crashing to her death. The truth is lost in time but it was food for thought.

Colin showed me around Toronto and informed me about

the geography and history of the place of which I knew very little. I was having such a good time there enjoying his hospitality that I stayed for two weeks, which was longer than I had intended, but in truth, I was making the most of extending my journey before settling down again. Travelling suited me better than settling.

He was a great host and he enjoyed having me there, asking me a lot about the home he was missing, but the time then came for me to resume my journey to cowboy land. I wanted to hitchhike the whole way across Canada to my destination some seventeen hundred miles away to properly see the land but that was probably a bit ambitious. Colin wouldn't hear of it. He flatly refused to let me do this saying my dad would never approve, and I suppose he was right. I couldn't convince him so I bought a ticket for the whole distance to Calgary. However, I had a plan.

Canada is such a vast country, that the scale doesn't easily compute to somebody from England. My journey to Calgary was enormous by English standards. I had already passed through the provinces of Nova Scotia, Quebec, and part of Ontario and would then need to cross the rest of Ontario, Manitoba, Saskatchewan and Alberta. From the time of landing in Montreal, it would take four days on the train to reach Calgary, a distance of about two thousand miles, crossing three time zones. So upon leaving Colin in Toronto, I still had three provinces ahead of me. And beyond Alberta was British Columbia where if you were so inclined you could dive into the Pacific Ocean. That enormous distance covers the land from East to West, but hundreds more miles go North until you hit the Arctic. The scale of the country is difficult to comprehend for someone from a small island. Canada is big!

Once I had settled on board the train from Toronto, I took advantage of the observation coach, the raised upper level of the carriage, surrounded by glass which gave a panoramic view of all that we passed. I was still on a roll with all of this. My spirits were still riding high. I was moving on, heading for pastures new.

As I watched the scenery passing by, on this first section through Ontario, it occurred to me that this was the land of the great Canadian humorist Stephen Leacock. I was a great fan of his writing and this was his country. I had come across his work in a small book called "Literary Lapses" in our school library, and though the tales were from a bygone age, his humour was timeless and human behaviour was the same. He had also written about his memories as a boy of the hard life on a farm in Upper Canada, as it was then called in the late eighteen hundreds, so it was of some interest to me to be cruising through his land on the train.

I was very receptive to all that was around me and was keenly taking in the scenery that we passed through. My first impression of this part of Ontario was that it looked like cowboy country. I seem to have been somewhat obsessed with cowboys. I suppose this was a combination of all the movies I had seen and what I had read about Western Canada. The landform of scrub and bush, hills, and boulders looked to my eyes raw and wild. I could visualize the posse on horseback chasing some black hats around those boulders, guns blazing, just like in the movies I had seen so many times as a boy. My imagination was running wild but the backdrop looked just right.

The train weaved its way along the North shore of Lake Superior, which was truly huge. Looking out across the water it was so vast that it was hard to believe it was just a lake and not an ocean. Ontario was very picturesque, with its lakes and hills, but as the journey progressed, the land gradually flattened out onto prairie as we approached Manitoba. And this land was really flat. Hardly a hill to be seen for miles. Clearly, the world was flat after all.

There was very little contrast in the scenery on the prairies. I saw grain elevators scattered across the land, some farms, a few small towns, and very straight roads. However, the names of the places that we passed through though were fascinating to me. Here I was seeing some quite exotic-sounding places in person, rather than just as names on a map in my school atlas. Some were obviously of Native American origin and some reflected their French history. We passed Winnipeg, Portage La Prairie, Regina, Moose Jaw, Swift Current, and many other smaller towns with interesting names.

Then after passing through Saskatchewan, we were into Alberta, and a town appeared with a name most intriguing of all to me, 'Medicine Hat'. That was a winner for me. So it was there that I took a bold step and left the train.

I had picked this place from studying the map, partly because it was not too distant from my destination of Calgary, about two hundred miles away, and partly because I couldn't resist the temptation of just having a look at a place with such an exotic-sounding name. 'Medicine Hat' conjured up images for me of the real West. I had decided to ditch the train, circumvent Colin's caution, and hitchhike the last leg of my journey. I was unencumbered by my cabin trunk which made its way without me to Calgary and my suitcase that Dad had found in his car was also following me on a separate journey. So once again it was just me and my old guitar.

I was keen to interact with the land and meet the people. So the train rolled on with one less passenger and I wandered up the High Street in this strangely named place to see what I might find.

I was now truly out in the 'Wild West'. Well maybe not so wild anymore, but the shadows of the true West and its history, and culture would surround me from that point on throughout my stay in Alberta. White cowboy hats were the preferred headgear there, along with jeans and boots, bootlace ties, and fancy embroidered shirts. The only things missing were six guns.

I strolled up the road taking it all in and the first thing to catch my eye was a Native American. A real-life Red Indian, sitting beside the road. I know that we now more respectfully call them First Nations, but back then my frame of reference was only from the Western Movies I had been brought up with as a boy. The word 'Indian' was not thought to be a derogatory term back then. So to me, they were still Red Indians.

Maybe he was a descendant of Sitting Bull, or White Cloud, or Geronimo, who knows? He looked every part like the guy the Cowboys were after. Perhaps I should introduce myself in the Indian way as, 'Travels with Old Guitar'? I was fascinated and also a bit cheeky. I said,

"Excuse me sir, but are you an Indian?" I don't know now how I had the nerve, but I did. "I've just arrived here from England and I've never met an Indian before." I thought I could get away with this line. I cannot remember his response. I believe that he just looked at me in bewilderment. Maybe he didn't understand my accent, but after a brief conversation, I carried on up the main road from the railway station.

I had a look around the central part of Medicine Hat, but despite its exotic name there wasn't much more to see or to interest me there. It was much like any other smaller town in Canada. There were no tepees, war dances, men bursting out of saloons, gunfights or mean-looking guys with black cowboy hats. Just a few shops and department stores. I soon had my fill. So having met Geronimo, I searched out the highway to try my luck at hitchhiking. Hitchhiking just seemed like an interesting way to get around. I didn't think about danger at all; so I set myself up by the roadside, thumb outstretched with a lot of hope.

The route from Medicine Hat to Calgary, like many routes in Canada, especially on the prairies consisted of one straight road connecting the two points, with not much in between except for a few grain elevators, homesteads with trucks in the driveways, and occasional small, one-horse towns on the roadside, all under that big, wide, prairie sky.

I did quite well at this, my first attempt at hitchhiking in Canada, and met a few people, swapped a few tales, and generally had a safe and pleasant final leg of my long journey from my distant home into the far West. I managed to get my last ride from an enormous truck, which took me right into Calgary. The truckers seemed to be the most friendly road users to hitchhikers, and many times I found that they were the ones who would stop for you, as the cars whizzed by, leaving you in a cloud of dust.

6

CALGARY

I had been travelling for three and a half weeks by the time I reached Calgary and the first thing to do was to try to find Auntie Grace's house in a city that was unknown to me. However, this was not difficult as the street layout is very logical with numbered streets going one way and numbered avenues going the other, so I found my way there without any difficulty. It was a typical Canadian older family-style wooden house with a staircase leading up from the ground level to the front door.

I was expecting a big welcome after my long journey from England, but that was pretty optimistic since I had taken so long in getting there because of my extended stay in Toronto, and my complete lack of communication. So nobody knew when I was going to arrive. A big welcome was probably a bit ambitious. I knew Auntie Grace but knew no one else there, so I knocked on the door and waited with some trepidation. I heard footsteps approaching and the door was opened by a man who was as much a stranger to me as I was to him, but he knew who I was.

"Hi! You must be Jim." (Yes, I suppose I must be.) It was Leo, a lodger and good friend of the family. He spoke with the slow drawl of a typical Westerner. "Welcome. Come on in. I'm Leo."

"Thanks, Leo, it's good to meet you. I'm afraid I got delayed for a while in Toronto."

Leo was a quiet, lovely, very gentle man, and in all the time that I knew him, I never once saw him get angry or move with any haste through life. He was a contented, unobtrusive, peaceful man, and was obviously the one wearing the white cowboy hat. Leo was a local Albertan, and he probably would have been breaking horses on a ranch in an earlier era, or roping steers or whatever it is that cowboys do to earn a crust. However, he did work at the cattle yards, a place steeped in Calgary's heritage as a cattle centre since its origins in the late nineteenth century. I make much of this cowboy angle but Calgary is at the heart of that culture and it assails you wherever you go in that region.

I asked after Auntie Grace, but Leo replied in his slow drawl, "Oh..., she's in England." This came as a surprise. "She found a cheap, last-minute flight deal and went last week." She had taken the opportunity to visit her large extended family there once more, so we had crossed paths on our journeys.

Auntie Grace had gone to Canada as a war bride and loved the country from the start. She had become a dedicated Canadian, but she enjoyed going back to England to visit her family so I had met her frequently over the years, and her message to us all was about the benefits of life in Canada. Nobody else from our family had yet made the venture. I was the first.

Travels with an old guitar

Leo welcomed me in, showed me around the house, and set about making me feel at home. The ground floor contained the lounge and dining areas, two bedrooms, a bathroom, and a kitchen, and from there, a staircase leading down to the lower level, or what was locally called "the rumpus room". This was the basement area but unlike English basements, it was not subterranean, as the main living area was elevated.

Rumpus rooms are very common in Canadian houses, and are a great recreational area, offering an alternative living space. They are great for a large family. This was where parties were often held and a place where the generations could separate to do their own thing. We had two extra bedrooms in this lower area, one for each of my cousins, Ron and Doug, and my bed was in the rumpus room, so each of us, Grace, Leo, Ron, Doug, and I each had our own space.

I was very comfortable in my new domain. I had plenty of room, with a television too. I would watch shows there that were quite new to me, like the Ed Sullivan Show, and others which acquainted me more closely with American culture of the time.

It was very nice having my own space. However, I did have to share the place with a monster, and that monstrous creature was the boiler for the central heating system, which is an essential feature of houses on the prairies. Winter conditions are much as I imagine the Arctic to be, as I was later to discover to my great shock. Every ten minutes or so, just as I was drifting off to sleep this great creature, which lived on the other side of a partition from me would wake me up again with a thunderous roar. I hated that thing from the first.

My cousin Ron was away at that time so I did not meet up with him for a few more weeks, and Doug would not be back from high school for a while, so once I had seen the house and taken it all in, I decided to go and have a look around the area, and check out the neighbourhood.

I found a couple of small shops and cafes nearby. It was very much a suburban residential area. The most notable difference to me was that the houses were all quite spacious and detached, nothing like the terraced houses that had been so common to me in England. I wasn't gone long on this exploration and by the time I returned school was out, so I met my cousin Doug for the first time.

Doug was 16 years old, a couple of years younger than me and still in school as were most of the kids of my age. I had been out to work already for a couple of years but school life went on longer in Canada than where I had come from and going on to higher education was also more common than it had been in my experience, so a lot of my new acquaintances were still in the education system.

I could see straight away that the culture Doug had grown from was very different from mine. He was another native Albertan, and I saw immediately how different we were. We are so much influenced by our background and surroundings in our youthful, formative years, and Doug and I were no exceptions.

The culture that I had come from for somebody of my age at that time of the early sixties, at least within my social group, entailed dressing in smart Italian suits and going to dances and pubs to socialise, but I now found myself in a very different place. The world I had entered, Doug's world, was a million miles from all of that.

Jim   Doug

Calgary

Drinking among my age group, at least in Alberta, had a very different aspect. For the young, it seemed to be a matter of getting drunk as fast as possible. That was the main attraction. This must have something to do with the strict liquor laws in Alberta.

The drinking age in Alberta was twenty-one and as I was only eighteen I was not even allowed to legally have a drink in a pub, or anywhere else for another three years. This was a blow for me as I had been going to pubs with my dad from a young age. I was later to find that the pubs, or "beer bars" in Canada too were rather strange. There were two entrances, one for men, and one for 'Ladies and Escorts' but both entrances led to the same place, an enormous room where, as you were not permitted to stand and drink, the beer was brought to you by waiters. The scale of it, like everything else, was very different. Ladies, it seemed, did not have the same freedoms as men. Why did men not also require escorts?

Doug informed me there was to be a school dance a few days hence, so he invited me to come along. It would be my first chance to get out and socialise, and to see how the natives lived, but I think Doug just wanted to show off his newly arrived English cousin. Fortunately, my suitcase had caught up with me by the time the dance came around, so I dressed in my Italian suit and tie, as was my custom, and off we went. It was a bad idea. I was clearly and unmistakably an alien. I might just as well have had a neon sign on me that read 'stranger`. All the other guys were dressed in jeans with chequered shirts and cowboy boots.

Travels with an old guitar

It was a million miles away from what I was accustomed to. I had got it completely wrong and must have looked quite odd to the locals. However, we did have fun. It was an eye-opener, the beginning of a learning curve and a reminder that I was now in a different cultural landscape, so the best thing for me to do would be to adjust. Maybe I should start with some jeans and cowboy boots?

There was also a young girl called Cathy who came to the house a day or two after I arrived. She was about my age, a friend of the family, who Auntie Grace had asked to call in and make sure I was alright when I arrived since I knew nobody.

And she did.

* * *

7

ALBERTA

I was in a position for a brief time then, before I set about finding a job, settling down, and joining the rat race, to continue being irresponsible and carefree, so I took the opportunity to get out on the road again. I decided to hitchhike to explore the surrounding territory.

I took the highway going South from Calgary, the Macleod Trail. It was very hot and uncomfortable on the roadside and a relief whenever I got a ride. Alberta is around 600 miles inland from the Pacific coast, so it has a continental climate. Although it gets ridiculously cold in the height of winter, the summers can be extremely hot. I did get several rides and after a time passing through Okotoks and High River, I reached the town of Fort Macleod just as it was starting to get dark.

When I think of it now I wonder how I was so careless about where I might sleep, or where I might be at the end of each day but I was young and didn't give it too much thought. I was carefree and just rolling along on the experiences of life without a worry in sight and certainly no responsibility. I was loving the freedom. Once more it was just me and the unknown road ahead, and those were always the best of times for me.

On this occasion, though I found refuge. As you entered the outer limits of the town, there was a mock-up fort which consisted of two wooden square enclosures, one on each side of the highway, as would have been on either side of the entrance of a true fort. It was about eight feet high with an open window section at about five feet. It looked like a safe unobserved place to sleep, so I threw my bag in and clambered up and over. It was open to the elements above, so not much hope if it rained, but at least I was surrounded by a wooden fortification. I was safe there from any carnivorous wildlife looking for an easy meal of wandering Englishman, and so was able to sleep for the night without incident.

The following morning after leaving the fort I first refreshed myself with some coffee at a cafe nearby and then continued travelling in a Southerly direction. I had a couple of short rides taking me a few miles along my way but then a longer, more interesting one.

An old, beaten-up pickup truck came smoking along the highway, stopped for me, and out stepped another Native American. This should not have surprised me as I was after all in their land. I climbed in, followed by the man and so was sandwiched between him and the driver, who was his brother.. They told me they were going as far as a town which, according to my map was directly on my route. This was perfect. So off we went. We talked a little, not very much, and drove on in relative silence. And then for want of conversation, I tried to engage with them and fell back on my old line once again.

"Are you two guys Indians? " I said. " I'm just here from England and I've never met an Indian before." They did not show any discomfort at being called 'Indians' but that was then.

"Yes." The driver said. That's it. He wasn't very talkative.

This line of conversation wasn't going far. I didn't want to offend the guys, but I thought to ask them what tribe they were from.

"The Blood Tribe." was the reply. I had never heard of the Blood Indians. They didn't feature in the old movies like the Sioux, the Cherokee or the Apache, and I could only assume that they got that name from some awful historical deeds. We drove on in silence for a while, and after a time they started talking to each other across me in their native language. What were they saying? What were they planning? I felt a little uneasy. The one turned to me then and said, "Hey, You wanna buy some moccasins? Our grandmother makes moccasins." Boy, what do I do now? I weighed up my options. I was foolishly brave.

"Err..No, thank you, but I don't want any moccasins."

We drove on and the silence continued as the miles rolled on. We didn't have much to talk about other than moccasins. I knew nothing about modern Native American ways although I would have loved to find out more but our conversation wasn't going that way, so I just admired the new scenery passing by. After a time we arrived at their town and they dropped me off. I thanked them and set off on foot once more.

I was getting thirsty, so decided to stop off at a cafe for a drink and maybe a hot dog without relish or something, so I made my way down the high street. This was a typical Western-looking town, a bit like I imagined the old West to be, with a main high street with shop frontages but not a cafe in sight that I could find.

I started walking down the street looking for one but gradually became aware that something was very wrong. I noticed that every face that I saw was Native American and they were all watching me as I walked by. Then it gradually dawned on me what it was. This was probably a reservation town and I had no business being there. No wonder they were all looking at me. I felt very uneasy with what seemed to be the whole of the Blood tribe watching my every move. They may not have been called that for nothing. They were probably very nice people but there was a large cultural gap between us that wasn't going to be bridged in my brief visit. I must have looked very unusual to them, strolling through their town. I thought better of my situation and decided that I had better keep moving and so turned around and went back up the high street to the highway to resume my journey. However, I had met the original people of this land. It would be good to get to know them more.

I set off on the road again, this time heading west in the direction of the Rockies. That whole region of Alberta is in the foothills of the Rockies, and I was on a road heading through one of the mountain passes toward British Columbia. This one was The Crowsnest Pass. I was doing well with getting rides in the right direction, and the further I went, the more mountainous the terrain became. The land was truly beautiful with soaring snow-covered mountains, valleys and icy streams that were so refreshing to drink from. I reached a place called Waterton Lakes and then turned North towards Pincher Creek where I once more set my sights on the West.

There were times when I would find myself on the roadside just outside of a town waiting for my next ride surrounded by all the majestic beauty of the Rockies, with peace all around me and just the birdsong to hear and the icy streams flowing out of the mountains. I would wonder then about my predicament should a bear amble out of the forest, as they sometimes do. I would have no escape, no refuge at all. Climbing a tree wouldn't do it. Mr Bear could easily catch me.

I came across a river there called the 'Oldman River' which amused me and set me to singing to the mountains, the river, and the birds.

Later in the day, a man pulled over to give me a ride and as we got chatting, he told me he was a local park warden. He asked me where I was heading, to which I had no sensible answer. I was heading West to nowhere. I was simply exploring. I was the 'delayed pioneer.' I should explain that this term comes from a Hungarian immigrant that I later worked with. There was a derogatory term that some used to refer to the many immigrants who came to Canada after the war and were referred to as D.P.s. This was an abbreviation of 'displaced persons.' My Hungarian friend Alex preferred the term "delayed pioneers."

It had begun to rain, the day was wearing on and my driver said that I would never get through the pass that night. I think he felt for my safety and my vulnerability. My situation was rather precarious, so he kindly invited me back to stay the night at his home with his wife and family. This was probably just what I needed at that time. It might even stop me from becoming bear food. So we drove on to his home, where he and his wife provided me with a meal, bed and comfort for the night. I was a stranger and yet they offered me the hospitality of their home, food, and a safe place to sleep. It was an unexpected kindness.

The family had two young boys and as we talked the evening away I got a real close-up view of one ordinary family and their lives for the first time as they enveloped me in their culture of hunting and living on the edge of the wilderness. This is what I had come for. I was as much of a curiosity to them too and they asked me lots of questions about England. They wouldn't have had many travellers such as me passing through their home. We spent a very pleasant evening swapping tales of our very different lives and the following morning they set me up with a good breakfast to see me on my way. People constantly surprise you.

The following morning I set off early and soon came across an interesting place just a little further down the road. The side of the hill was littered with huge boulders and the sign on the side of the road told me that this was the site of the former town of Frank, but sadly it was no more. The town was obliterated in 1903 when half of the mountainside fell, burying it, and taking out the Canadian Pacific railway line in one of the biggest slides of all time in Canada. There is nothing there now except for rubble and the sign.

Alberta

This little hitchhiking diversion, though brief, was interesting and it gave me a small taste of life in Canada, The West, and the people. I had reached the town of Fernie, inside British Columbia and had planned to take the route North to Banff after a few more miles and then turn back East making a circuit back to Calgary. That was starting to seem a little ambitious and I realised that I ought to turn round and head back to Calgary if I was to be in time to meet up with Auntie Grace on her return from England. She had planned a weekend drive to Vancouver on the West Coast to visit family friends and this was a trip I didn't want to miss, so I turned around and headed back towards Fort Macleod

My journey back to Calgary must have been quite uneventful because I can't remember any of it. Not one single incident

8

STAMPEDE

Back in Calgary, I at last linked up with Auntie Grace and it was lovely to catch up with her again. She had had a great time in England visiting family as she always did. Grace was very much a people person and on those trips, she would make a point of singling out every person in the family to engage with one-to-one and that's why I already knew her so well. She loved Canada but she also loved her whole extended family. My dad had been asking how I was, but of course, she didn't know. She had to tell them that she hadn't even seen me yet, as I had gone walkabout in Toronto. I had not been a good communicator. I was just tumbling along with the old tumbleweed.

Auntie Grace was a tiny lady with a huge presence, and like so many in my family, she always had plenty to say. We were to have many friendly arguments over the next few months about haircuts, England vs. Canada, clothes and such, and especially the climate as the winter came on, but they were just friendly banter, which we both enjoyed. She was a lovely lady and was to be like a second mother to me. She welcomed me into her home along with everybody else there.

She had had a life with many trials and was to have many

more over the years. She endured things that would have broken many people, but like many in my family, she was very religious and her faith carried her through them all.

She had gone to Canada as a war bride and met with real hardship right away. Her husband was an alcoholic and would disappear for days at a time leaving her to cope as best she could with her two young boys. He eventually drank himself to death at the age of just forty, leaving her to fend for herself. Her first grandson, less than a year old, was later to have an accident and strangle himself by jumping up and down in the cot, and sadly there was more heartache to come for her, which I will describe a little later. These were terrible things for her to have to endure, but despite all the hardships, she somehow maintained a great spirit of happiness.

She loved dancing and had a large collection of old Country records, which were standard fare in that part of the world, but they were new to me, so I spent many hours poring over the covers and playing them. I loved the music, though I had never heard of most of those Country artists before.

Auntie Grace had only been home for a few days when she, Leo, Doug, and I set out for a long weekend trip to Vancouver, some 600 miles away, in their old Rambler car. That was a pretty enormous journey by my scale of reference for just a three-day trip but things were different in Canada. The journey had been much improved, so they told me, since the opening of the Rogers Pass, but even so, it was still a mighty journey in my eyes.

I saw the Rockies now from many viewpoints, high and low and they were truly magnificent. I had never seen such amazing scenery as we motored past glacial valleys, high snow-covered peaks and raging rivers. Auntie Grace told of when she had gone camping up there with her husband and two small boys. One day she came across a bear going through their stuff and managed to shoo him away. Pretty brave stuff I would say.

We stopped periodically to grab a hamburger for sustenance, and after a long drive reached our destination on the coast. This was my first view of Vancouver which is a beautiful city close to the mountains and the sea. I would get to know it very well in the future.

Grace's friends welcomed us with more food and grand hospitality and we were able to see a little of the town, but mostly this was a social visit, so we spent much of the time just talking and catching up. We had a couple of days enjoying ourselves there and once again for me, it had been a time to see how Canadians lived. It struck me that in general, they were happy people, and maybe the environment had something to do with it. Canada is an uncrowded place with plenty of room for all which I think seemed to inspire optimism. There was very much a "can do" attitude which was refreshingly different from the feeling that prevailed in England. Those were the sort of impressions that I was getting. So in no time at all, we were again Alberta-bound and were soon home in Calgary. I had come a very long way from my familiar world in Brighton and it was a fascinating experience to integrate myself into a new way of life.

Since leaving England, I had led a carefree, irresponsible life of moving at my own pace wherever I chose. It was the life that I loved best, but now the time had come when I had to knuckle down and try to find a job to support myself. I couldn't keep wandering around forever. Or could I? So it was back to the reality of ordinary life.

I began by phoning around a lot of companies using the yellow pages to see if I could find any openings as well as registering myself at the employment agency. I didn't have much to offer to a prospective employer, as my experience was limited up until that point in my life. I had worked as a very junior person in a lawyer's office, so my only real experience had been in a clerical position. However, jobs were plentiful and I managed to find an opening in the small subsidiary office of a steel plant where they made snowmobiles. I was in the branch where they held all the raw materials of steel and that's where I met the aforementioned Alex, the Hungarian.

The company just needed someone to be there to look after things, so I had a small office of my own with very little to do, but it was a job. Although I wasn't required to do very much, the wage was ten times what I would earn in England. It was in a rural part of town close to the open country and I would often look out of my office window and be amused to see the little gophers pop their heads above the ground periodically before diving underground again.

Our household now consisted of Auntie Grace, Leo the lodger, my two cousins Ron and Doug, and myself, but often the house was full, with not only us, but the many friends of my cousin Ron. If any occasion came around such as a birthday, Thanksgiving, Easter, or almost any other thing at all we would gather and feast ourselves on buckets of Kentucky

Travels with an old guitar

Fried Chicken. I must have been a lot cheekier in those days because I can remember at least once going into the KFC place and announcing to the staff and my audience in my best put-on English upper-class accent, "Would you please go and tell the Colonel that I'm here."

I got to know Ron's pals well, and soon just became one of the crowd. It often brought home to me again those cultural differences between us when we all got together. I tried to go native and blend in with them and did so quite well. They accepted me into the gang but they were motivated by completely different things from me. Being a really tough guy, and who could beat up who was all-important to them, but it was something that had no meaning for me at all. For all of my life, I had shied away from violence and wanted no part of it. I came to realise in the end that is the way things are with young males in rural North America.

But despite that difference between us, we socialised well together and I tried to adjust to my new surroundings. It was a learning process. I remember one of Ron's buddies named 'Coon' that I got on with very well. He was called this on account of the permanent very dark shadows around his eyes making him look like a raccoon. Coon always called me 'Teabag,' on account of my drinking preference. We would often hang around together when Ron was not about, and he was very interested in England, which was a world away from his own. I was experiencing a completely different culture from mine throughout this early time in Canada as an alien, but of course, the people that I met and talked to were also seeing a foreign world through me. I found that I could often raise good entertainment among them by really laying on and exaggerating my English accent, sometimes becoming very upper-class, sometimes the opposite, so colloquial that it left them looking quite bewildered. I was just having fun with them.

Calgary has been a cowboy town since its beginning when it started life as a cattle centre, and that aspect of its history remains an influence today. Before I began my journey there, I had heard of the one big event that puts the town on the map: The Calgary Stampede, which is probably the biggest rodeo in North America. It is held at the beginning of July each year, and is a huge event, attracting people from across the world. The Stampede grounds occupy a corner of the town where the rodeo events are held.

In the main arena, they hold chuck-wagon races, steer-roping, and fancy horse riding events, where brave cowboys try to stay on horses that don't want them there. There are cattle and livestock displays, fairground attractions, and more. The event has grown into something much more than just a rodeo.

The local native tribes, the Blackfoot, the Cree, and the Stoney come into town, where they set up tepees and create an Indian village inside the stampede grounds. There were the guys I had seen many times in my childhood on the big silver screen. Their features were unmistakable, all dressed in their brightly coloured beaded buckskin clothes, with their children, looking adorable as smaller versions of their parents.

The Indians, or as I should now properly call them 'First

Nations,' were fascinating to me.

Two big chiefs.

Also within the Stampede grounds was 'the midway,' where there are sideshows, food stalls, amusements, crazy rides designed to bring back your lunch, freak shows, and all the usual fairground amusements. As I wandered around taking all this in I had no idea that the following year I would be a part of the entertainment myself, playing music with my band.

During stampede week, if you get up early enough in the morning, a visit downtown would reward you with a free breakfast of pancakes, eggs, and bacon served from chuck wagons on the side of the street. Traffic is kept away and the whole downtown area is devoted to the celebrations, with square dancing in the streets to banjo and fiddle bands. There was a great spirit of celebration everywhere. Calgary people will tell you that their city is at the top when it comes to

Stampede

hospitality, and I wouldn't dispute the truth of that. To begin the week's celebrations, a parade weaves its way through town, with the acts and performers from the shows, the chuck wagons, horses, cattle, cowboys, Mounties, and Native Americans, all dressed in their finest clothes. It is a very impressive, colourful display, and of course, maple leaf flags are everywhere.

I would often go to the stampede with cousin Doug, and although he had been born and grew up in Calgary, and had seen all of this before, he still enjoyed it as much as I did. The excitement had never paled for him. When he was younger he had had a role in the parade following behind with a shovel to pick up the horse droppings, which he told me brought large cheers from the crowd.

One day, while walking through the midway, on an impulse, I paid my money to visit the freak show where, once inside the tent, I saw many curiosities including the 'crocodile woman' with scaly skin, a bearded lady, a tiny man, barely three feet tall called Tom Thumb, a woman who passed electric currents through her body, and various other strange sights. But the scariest of them all was a man going under the name of "Popeye". His act is all in his name, and standing in the front, just underneath him, was not the best place to be. That was a scary one. The Midway was an exciting place full of activity and, the Calgary Stampede was a great experience for me.

However, my new housemate Leo, a native cowboy at heart, with his cowboy hat, embroidered shirt, bootlace tie, boots, and jeans, wanted me to see the real thing. He believed that the Calgary Stampede was too large, too commercial, and not at all like the real thing. So a few weeks later, he drove me to a small town called High River to see their annual smaller-scale rodeo, which in his opinion, was in the true spirit of rodeos, where we could see the action up close. There we sat astride a fence, which was often battered by horses, as we watched the bronco riding just a few feet below us. We hung on tightly in case we ended up as a part of the action ourselves. Those cowboys certainly earned their money, putting their lives in such danger. When the action came close to crushing our feet, we would have to scramble up on the fence a bit more for our safety.

There were all the same rodeo events as in Calgary: the chuck-wagon races, steer-roping, and all the rest, but we were right on top of the action. These events were all performed by professional rough riders who made a living travelling from rodeo to rodeo. Later, in my hitchhiking travels, I would meet a couple of them myself as they moved from town to town with their saddles and gear in the back of their car. After the main shows, Leo and I walked around among the cattle, alongside a group of huge scraggly-haired buffalo. They were quite imposing but very tame and unflustered by the people walking among them. It was all a very different experience for an English boy a long way from home.

During my time in Calgary, I tried my hand at one or two different jobs. One of these was working in the office of a flour mill just outside of town, and it was there that I first encountered the 'Hutterites.' These were people who lived in a separate community, rather like the Amish people and the Mennonites. They were a sect that had originated in Europe and migrated to North America in the previous century. They lived in comparative isolation from the main centres in Canada, living a largely independent self-sufficient existence, but they would visit the flour mill to trade. They stood out whenever you saw them as they always dressed in their traditional way: the men and the boys always with braces for their trousers and broad-brimmed hats and the women and girls wearing bonnets.

While I was working at the flour mill I saw them come to visit and trade several times. Some years later, I got to know a man who had grown up in one of those communities and he amused us by telling the tale that he had to have a shirt made from a 'Robin Hood' flour sack. This was the name of the flour manufacturer, so he had to go around with 'Robin Hood' written on his back, which must have amused people.

Until I went to Canada, I had never experienced 'Drive-in' restaurants, so they were quite unknown to me, but they were a way of life there. The system was that you drove in, turned your lights on, and a waitress would come to your car, take your order and bring it to you. One day I was at the local 'A and W' in a friend's car when the young waitress came to take our order. I found, not for the first time, that the girls would be quite taken with my accent. I got chatting with her. Her name was Sandy and before I knew it I had a date. She was a lovely girl and we went out together for a short while. It was just a brief interlude and I cannot remember how it ended but it did and life moved on.

Travels with an old guitar

Jim   Sandy

All in all, I liked what I had found and was happy to adapt to this world that I had come to, although it was very different in so many ways from my life experiences up until that point. I believed I had made the right choice in going there, but I often thought of home and would avidly watch for the postman and took great delight in the many letters I received from my family and friends in England.

And then a series of exciting things happened to make my life much more interesting.

9

THE BAND

My aunt and two cousins had made me very welcome in Calgary, but I had practically no friends or acquaintances of my own, and I was an alien at that. I needed to get out and meet people, and as playing the guitar had always been a love of mine, I could use that to help me and perhaps get into a local band. I had played bass guitar with a band in England, and in the nineteen sixties, English music was making a storm around the world. This was due to the manic popularity of the Beatles, The Rolling Stones, and others. They were calling it 'The British Invasion' and that was the music I had been playing back home, so this was just the right time for me. Being English was a real asset in the music world, and a Beatle haircut helped even more.

So, through an acquaintance of Auntie Grace, I was given an introduction to a guy who had a small pop group. I went to meet him and his band and it all went very well, which resulted in them welcoming me in to join them as their bass player. I started going to their practices and was very excited about this new development in my life. I was making connections, and better still, it was through my music.

Unfortunately, though, I soon realised that the music they

were playing was not to my liking at all. They were just doing guitar tunes with twangy guitars and playing the Surf Music that was coming out of California at that time. It was good enough, I suppose in its way, with clever little guitar riffs, but it was not my thing at all. I was glad to be playing again, but it was not exactly what I wanted. I had just come from England where Rhythm and Blues music was far more exciting to play. As a bass player, you could put some real feeling into the music, unlike the stuff that these guys were playing, which I found to be quite monotonous. So, my little stint with them did not last long and shortly thereafter I abandoned that band.

However, soon after that little episode, a chance meeting occurred that was to lead me in a direction that was much more to my liking. I needed a haircut, or at least a slight trim. My hair was not very long as far as I was concerned, but it was long by the local standards where the guys of my age had really short hair, just like their fathers and their fathers before them. The sixties hadn't quite arrived in Alberta. I had already triggered strange looks from people at work who were not accustomed to men who had more than half an inch of hair on their heads. So I took a trip downtown, picked a suitable-looking men's hairdresser, and walked in.

I found out later that all of the guys in the backroom had been drawing lots on who would be the unlucky one to cut the hair of this long-haired stranger, and the short straw was drawn by a man called Terry. As he attacked my hair, with me ever watchful for him to go easy, we talked, and I found that he was also a guitar player and had played with several of the local bands. We made an immediate connection and arranged to meet up later. It had been a chance meeting that led to a great new adventure for me. Terry and I became very good friends and spent many hours playing music together. We formed a band and although we have lived far apart for a long time now, we are still in touch.

A few weeks later, we were checking out guitars in a music shop when another friend of his came in. He was a big guy with a big voice, and I was immediately impressed when he started singing. He was a class act with a lot of charisma which would carry him a long way. He would subsequently go on to have great success and fame in his own right with a solo career both in Canada and England. His name was Keith Hampshire and a couple of years after this meeting in the guitar shop and what that led to, he went to England where he got a job as a DJ on the pirate ship 'Radio Caroline'. He gained a lot of recognition in Britain, and then, after returning to Canada, he had a couple of number-one hits there and hit the charts in the USA. Keith was a very talented singer and actor, and I saw him some years later as a resident, playing comical roles on a Canadian TV comedy show. But that was all in Keith's unknown, unwritten future the day that we met in the guitar shop.

Between the three of us, we had the makings of a great new group. We got on well together, which was very important for any band, but the main thing that we had in common was that we were all keen to play the latest music coming from England by groups like Manfred Mann, The Animals, The Rolling Stones, and others. The days of just standing in a row strumming and picking guitars to sweet songs by somebody called Bobby were over. Now there was music that you could put some soul into. I knew some great songs that they had not heard, which they took to with great enthusiasm. Then through Keith and Terry's musical connections, we acquired a drummer, a keyboard player, and a rhythm guitar player, which made us complete.

We went under the name of 'Keith and The Variations.' We blended well, had a great sound, and soon started getting bookings for dances, social events, and weddings. We became very popular and were a good band with the talented Keith upfront, who knew how to work an audience, Terry, a first-class lead guitar player, and the English bass player with the Beatle haircut.

Some interesting gigs came our way. We played one time for a wedding reception in the penthouse of a top hotel in Calgary, where we were fed with the best steaks that I ever tasted. After all, this was Alberta, the heart of cattle country. I was told that for the last few weeks of their lives, the cows were fed on beer. We had regular bookings at several dance venues in town and were making a name for ourselves. Dressed in the neat camel-coloured jackets with black lapels we had made for us, we were a smart act.

Keith had a daytime job as a cameraman at CFCN, the local TV station. This meant he was in exactly the right place when he heard that the station was looking for a band to be resident on a pop music show to be broadcast bi-weekly on Saturdays. We welcomed the chance of this as it would give us added exposure, and as a result, we were soon playing regularly and being broadcast on the local TV station. The show was a pop and dance programme aimed at the teenage and young adult audience. The format was record playing, and dancing, interspersed with our band performing. The show was compered by a talented host by the name of Don Wood. It was broadcast locally but was also syndicated to other TV stations in cities across Canada, so we were getting wide coverage across the country.

Keith and the Variations.
Gerry, Keith, Terry, Doug, Jimmy, Art

The Band

So, all of this meant that for the next year or so, times were great for me. I had only been in Canada for a few months and suddenly it was all happening. It was exciting and amazing, and I enjoyed some of the best times I have ever had.

The shows were always recorded and usually went out live, but sometimes they were broadcast locally a few hours later. When this happened, we would go to one of our homes and watch ourselves on TV, which I found to be a very weird experience. Many years later, I wrote to CFCN to see whether those tapes still existed, as it would be fascinating to look back and see my younger self, and my kids would be greatly amused I'm sure. But in those days, the tapes on the very expensive reel-to-reel machines were re-used over and over again, so, unfortunately, those recordings, like so many things, are long gone. But there lives in the back of my mind the faint hope that somewhere in a dusty archive cupboard in one of those Canadian TV stations, buried under all the other junk, there may be one of those tapes, though it's pretty certain that I will never know.

We became quite well known in the local area, because of the TV shows, to the point where I would sometimes be recognised as I went about my normal life, and that was something that I did not like at all. I just wanted to be anonymous. Keith was our greatest asset and he deserved the attention, but the compere of the show would often play up to my English background. He would ask me things about music out of the blue while we were on the air. The Beatles had drawn great attention to anything British, but all I wanted to do was to be a part of the band and play bass, nothing more. I loved playing Bass and was just in it for the music

I had bought myself an amp and a bass guitar to play with the band but was very taken with a beautiful Gibson guitar that I had seen in a music shop. It was quite beyond the limits of my finances at the time, but Keith knew of a good Luthier in town so he took me over to meet him. I arranged to have a customised bass guitar made for me, very similar to the Gibson. He was a master craftsman and made me the nicest instrument I have ever owned, made to my specifications.

When we had finished playing at a dance, we would often go to a Mexican restaurant or a pizza place late at night to unwind from the exhilaration of the evening, and it was then that I discovered pizza for the first time. Pizza is commonplace everywhere now, but at that time it had not yet arrived back in my hometown in England, and I loved it. I swore right then that if there was a heaven and I went there, it would be to eat pizza for eternity. God might tire of it but I wouldn't.

We had a manager by the name of Stu, who had a little white Triumph Spitfire car. He was quite adept at sliding sideways around corners in the snow which was a bit unnerving for me as a passenger.

We became friendly with a family of English girls at that time, who had recently come to Canada and we would often go to their house after a dance and stay half the night playing music with acoustic guitars. It was a great relaxing come-down after the loud amplified electric music that we had been playing.

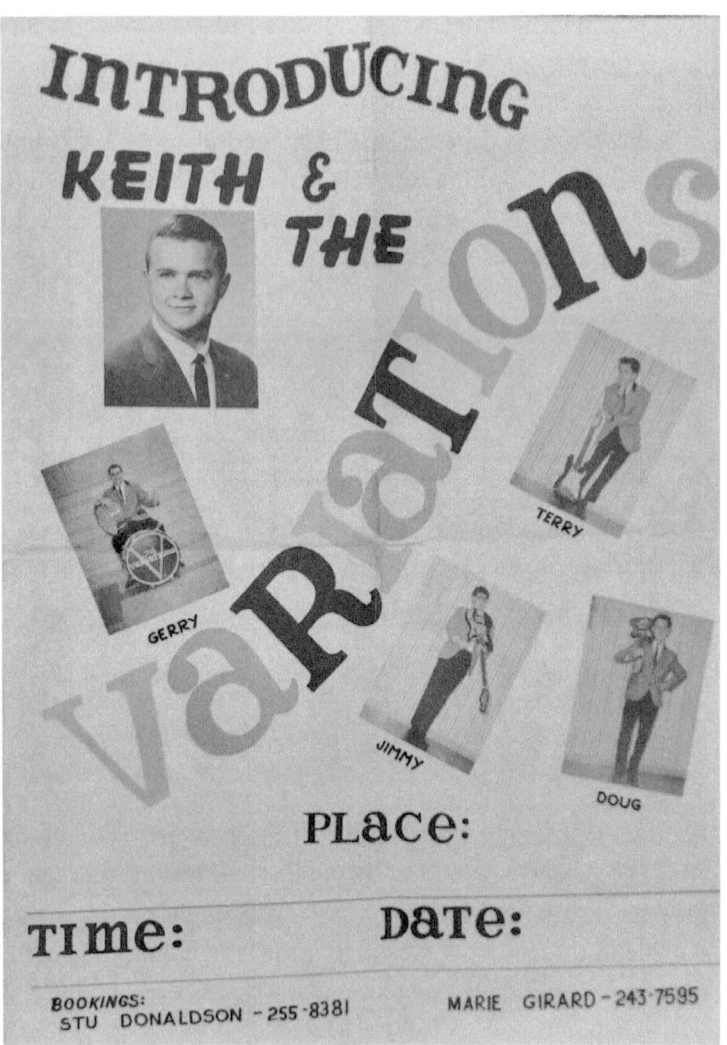

The Band

There were often girls who were keen to hang out with us. 'Groupies' I suppose, but perhaps that's just one of the things that go with the territory of being great TV stars. (Ho Ho).

This involvement with the band was exciting and a great deal of fun, but there were some experiences that I had while it was happening which I found quite stressful.

One time, as the show was underway, Don, the compere announced,

"Hey, guys! Who wants to hear Jimmy Brown sing, 'Mrs. Brown, you've got a lovely daughter?'" It was a popular song at the time by the group, Herman's Hermits. I was in shock. We knew the song as a band, but I wasn't the singer and I barely knew the lyrics. Don played some records and chatted while we had a quick rehearsal, and then I was thrust into the spotlight against my will to sing the song before the cameras. It was not my happiest moment.

On another occasion, we were playing at the opening of a new club with Don, as usual, being the compere. We played a few numbers between records, and then as I was walking past him during a commercial break, he grabbed me and asked me to do a live interview about the band and the music.

"No, no Don!" I said. "Not me. I have no idea what to say."

"Don't worry Jimmy," he said. "I'll just feed you lines."

The ad break finished and then amidst all the noise, the cameras came back on, and I found myself sitting there with Don, acting a role, pretending that I knew all about the music scene in England. I just uttered whatever came into my head, which was probably nonsense, while thinking "Why am I here? How did I get into this?" as the camera looked on silently, watching and listening. It made me very nervous, but when I watched the playbacks I couldn't see that nervousness, so it seems my little bit of acting worked.

The result of all this exposure led to something else that I didn't expect. I started to get letters from young girls all across Canada. Fan mail, no less. It was all pretty crazy, and the guys in the band of course teased me no end as I read them at the studio where they had been delivered. I remember after reading one, Terry putting his arm around me and whispering in my ear, "Oh, Jimmy! If only we could just be alone together somewhere", a phrase that was in one of the letters

I remember all of this because the experience of the TV shows was quite nerve-wracking for me. Keith thrived on it, and he was good at it, but it just wasn't my thing. I never wanted to be a frontman, a spokesman for my group, or my country. I found the presence of the TV camera looking at me, with unknown numbers of watchers on the other side quite unnerving. I didn't mind a live audience. The audience response and feedback were a big part of how our music came across, but the TV camera was a silent ominous presence with its huge all-seeing Cyclops eye. An audience would respond. That thing did not. It just watched you in silence. Many young people seem to crave that attention, but it wasn't for me. I had a small taste of it and I am glad I did, but it didn't suit me. I didn't like the spotlight and just wanted anonymity.

I suppose, in looking back on it, I was somewhat conflicted between the thrill and excitement of being in the band playing regularly on TV and a desire for a quiet life and not being recognised.

However, the overall experience of those days will always remain a great memory for me. I had a fantastic time.

* * *

10

GAYLE

Then I met Gayle.

It is more than fifty years now since I met Gayle but I still remember it well. Our band was booked to play at a dance at the Haysboro Community Centre in Calgary. We were hauling in our heavy amps, drums, and equipment and setting up. Gayle was there helping to set things up in the hall and, I became aware of her as she kept looking at me. She was very young, but young or not, she had that instinctive womanly way of looking at a man that captivates him. No chance for me at all.

I whispered to Keith, "Hey Keith, look at that lovely young girl over there. She keeps giving me the eye."

"Oh," said Keith. He was quite disinterested.

"Well, she's rather gorgeous but she looks very young. What do you think Keith? What should I do?"

"Jimmy – Just go for it!" he said. And so for the rest of the evening, we made eyes at each other. Something was happening.

Sometimes in life incidents occur that have far-reaching effects that we don't realise at the time and this was one of them. Gayle was to impact upon my life in a profound way that would affect me for the rest of my life, though at the time I could not have known that. She was just a girl in the audience, and I was just the bass man in a band.

We talked in the interval and after the dance. The sparks were flying. So we arranged to meet on a date, and this was followed by several more. Time went on and we became very close and shared a wonderful feeling of togetherness. It was the first love for both of us and was quite amazing. It was never to be forgotten by either of us. I hadn't expected this. It had just come from nowhere. We had captured something beautiful together, and we would never forget the deep love that we shared. It was the beginning of a long and intricate story, with some surprising and unexpected turns, but I must deal with them one stage at a time.

I met her family, her parents, Phil and Jeannette, her two younger sisters, and her brother, and they seemed to like and accept me. Phil was a great character who I liked and admired. He and I had a natural connection as he also played the guitar and sang some great old cowboy songs, although I trod with some caution of course. He was Gayle's dad, after all.

Much later, I was to learn of his exploits during the war when he had landed on the beaches at Juno with the Canadian troops. He experienced some very frightening times, running up the beach while his fellows were being gunned down all around him. He had some amazing stories to tell. One time, he was hiding within feet of the German soldiers that he could hear talking just beyond the bushes above him. Gayle recognised the value of his stories and fortunately, she was able to record him reciting some of them later in his life.

Gayle

I'm sure that he must have been teasing me when one day he threw this at me out of the blue."You know Jimmy, life revolves around sex." How could I respond? How do you answer that from your girlfriend's dad? There I was taking up with his very young daughter when he threw that one at me. He was a man with an ever-present twinkle in his eye, and I would have liked to have gotten to know him better. I think that we had a lot in common.

He did tell me once that he thought I was very brave to have come on this adventure to Canada all on my own at the age of eighteen, but that was nothing when compared with his wartime experiences when the bullets were flying all around him and his buddies were falling.

So, Gayle and I went merrily on with our courtship for several months and it was wonderful. We were devoted to each other, but one day after I had been visiting with them and having a great time, her mum and dad drove me home. When we got there they stopped the car and her dad threw another surprise at me quite unexpectedly. I was in the back of the car with Gayle, and he turned round to me and said."Jimmy, we like you. You are a great guy but we think that you are a bit too old for Gayle, and don't think you two should carry on seeing each other."

Gayle and I were both dumbfounded. She didn't know it was coming either. There was a mere two years between us and we thought the world of each other. Of course, we simply ignored him. Wouldn't you? The magnetic force between us was too strong.

The climate in Alberta, and all across the prairies in the wintertime, is awful. In my opinion, it doesn't seem to be suitable for fragile humans. There is a line in the song by Ian Tyson, "Four Strong Winds" that goes "...Think I'll go out to Alberta, weather's good there in the fall." Well, great song Ian, but I cannot agree. The weather was just plain horrible in my opinion. It gets very, very cold, often down to forty below zero, so it was quite a shock to me when the winter arrived in full force. It felt like my brain and blood were beginning to freeze, and I began to wonder what I was doing there. It gets so cold that running is dangerous as it can freeze the lungs. Children are warned not to touch the metalwork of a car, as it could tear their skin if they pulled their hand away.

Long Johns and earmuffs, a hat, gloves, and six coats are essential for life. I couldn't quite believe how cold, cold can be. I was working in the office near Gopher City and after a long walk to get there, when I took my glasses off to clean them, one arm just snapped clean off because it was so cold and brittle. It was a long way from those tropical beaches that had set me travelling.

So one day, when I came home freezing and stamping the snow off my shoes I said to Auntie Grace, "This is just plain ridiculous! How can a body survive this? "

"Oh, it's just bracing." she said. Grace would defend Calgary to the hilt.

"Bracing? No. It's just freezing my balls off." I said. "I'm going to California."

"Oh no, you're not." She replied, "When you came here, you said you would stay for a year, and that's what you will do."

I couldn't remember having made such a promise, but I suppose I must have done so, otherwise she wouldn't have said it, so I had to submit. Well if I lived until the springtime I would be a happy man. Meantime, it was Long Johns, ear muffs, sturdy shirts and jumpers, a large coat and some kind of substantial hat, and I was still cold.

Calgary was a big sprawled-out city so I needed to get myself a car and start driving. So one day I phoned Keith to ask for his help. Cars were pretty cheap then, especially old ones and there were plenty of used car lots, so he came over and we set off on our search. After wandering around looking at a few, we found a 1954 Ford. It was a monster with a big 8-cylinder engine, a bench seat in the front (ideal for snuggling up to a girlfriend), an automatic transmission and a radio. An ideal first car, and within my very limited budget. It cost me thirty-five dollars. Unfortunately, the car didn't make it home! It overheated on the way there, but that turned out to be just the water pump, so when that was fixed I was away and mobile. Everything else worked fine. Things were getting better all the time. It would swallow gas in vast quantities and a visit to my pal Terry, who lived on the other side of town, seemed to take almost a tank full, but gas was extremely cheap back then.

I rapidly got to love my monstrous old car. One time I was due to pick up Gayle at the bus loop and I was late. It was way below zero, and the poor girl was nearly frozen to death by the time I got there, but she was there waiting and refused to give up on me.

Another new thing to me was drive-in movies. They were commonplace throughout North America at that time. Often, they would run a series of horror movies lasting the whole night long, and on those nights, it was a gathering place for our young generation.

The cars would park up in rows, each beside a post and from it, you would pull in a speaker to hang on the inside of the window. Usually, these were so distorted as to be almost indecipherable if they worked at all. They were somewhere below the low end of lo-fi. At the end of the evening, you had to try to remember to put the speaker back onto the post, but unfortunately, this was often forgotten until the wire snapped as you drove away.

The movie, however, was unimportant. The object of the exercise was not to watch the movie at all but to climb into the backseat with your nice warm girlfriend. That was the main aim for us adolescents whose hormones ruled everything. Where else could we go?

There was a drawback to all of this though. In winter, in that part of the world, the plummeting temperature would creep into the car after a while and you would have to turn on the engine to get the heater working. So the evening was filled with the sound of cars starting up every few minutes. The drive-in movies were very popular and there were a lot of them scattered around the city. They are probably all long gone by now, but I am glad that I did get to experience them while they were there.

This was all great fun for me, as I absorbed it all and assimilated into the Canadian culture. I was having a ball, and I loved the luxury of being independent and driving myself around in my big luxurious car, but my driving experiences came to an abrupt end. With the winter came the snow and ice and I was a new, inexperienced driver. I had not yet learned the caution that comes with age and experience.

One eventful evening, I was driving to play at a dance with the band. Gayle was beside me, and in the back of the car were cousin Doug and Mary June, a friend of Gayle's who was there as a blind date for Doug. The traffic was creeping along very slowly but there was an empty unused lane beside me. I thought I could pass them all if I just sneaked into that one. But as soon as I had moved over, it became obvious why the lane had remained empty. It was covered with sheer ice. I lost control right away, but by then it was too late. I tried to correct the steering but it was beyond capture as we swerved left and right all over the road, fortunately not colliding with any other vehicles.

We came to a sudden halt as the car collided sideways with a lamppost. The side of the car collapsed and compressed around my legs, fortunately, without crushing them or breaking any of my bits. Gayle was thrown against me and the back door flew off, followed by Doug, followed by Mary June, who landed on top of him, which was a surprising first date for them both. Mary June's take on this when she told it with some amusement is that she 'flew out of there like Mary Poppins.'

The car was beyond repair, so that was the end of my driving for a while. We made a phone call and Gayle and I got picked up to continue to the dance, and Doug was taken to the hospital with a concussion but with no serious injuries. I got it in the neck from Auntie Grace later as she heard a report of the accident with Doug's name mentioned on the radio. I don't remember what happened to Mary June. I only hope that we didn't leave her lying on the road. It was quite a night for us all.

Winter had come and with it my first Christmas in Canada. I found an Indian artefacts shop downtown that sold moccasins, tomahawks, and various other beaded things, so I bought a whole load of these and parcelled them up to send to my family back home. I heard later that this gave them great amusement. Ronn was a-whooping it up with a tomahawk playing the Indian on a war dance.

Travels with an old guitar

So after a long cold winter, eventually springtime arrived and I was still breathing, and then it was summer. It all seemed wonderful. It was Stampede week again, and I was there for the second year. There is a guest of honour in the parade each year, and on this occasion, it was my immense pleasure to see Walt Disney pass by just a few feet away in an open-top car waving to the crowd. What an honour to see the man who was responsible for bringing such happiness and laughter to us children throughout the world.

Our band was playing that year at the stampede grounds along with various other groups. There were huge crowds everywhere. The smell of hot dogs and popcorn pervaded the air, and the noise of the rides and the screaming of excited kids as we emerged onto a raised stage to entertain. It was our big moment. I have to say, it felt pretty good to look down and see the crowd and to give them our best music. The pop world had invaded. Keith told me years later that we were playing on the same bill as Roy Orbison, but that has simply dropped out of my memory altogether, so I am not even sure that it happened although he assures me that it did.

I had thought that having an Auntie Grace probably put me in a fairly exclusive club, but no, I was wrong. One day Keith came round to see me and told me that he also had an Auntie Grace who lived in Saskatoon, Saskatchewan and he was planning to visit her. He asked me if I would like to tag along. It sounded like a fun trip, so a few days later we loaded up his little convertible sports car and hit the road heading East. Saskatoon is around four hundred miles or about six hours of driving from Calgary on those very straight prairie roads.

It was a long and uneventful drive across the flatland thereabouts, but there is one interesting place that we passed, called Drumheller, which is well-known for its rich fossil finds from the Jurassic and Cretaceous times. I had always had an interest in dinosaurs, like most boys, and Drumheller was just littered with their fossil bones. We did not have the time just then to search among the rocks, but we pulled off the road to see the area of 'The Badlands' as they are known, where the land drops away into deep gorges and canyons. Given more time, we would have poked around and I'm sure we would have found something, as the bones are so numerous. It would be great to return there sometime and explore the place properly.

Eventually, after a long, long, tiring drive across the prairies of Alberta and Saskatchewan, we arrived at the home of this other Auntie Grace. She was a sweet., elderly lady, who was very glad to see her nephew Keith. She made us very welcome and set about feeding us, as Aunties do. This Auntie Grace, like mine, had also had tragedies in her life. Keith warned me not to ask too many questions concerning the family.

Her particular tragedy was as follows. Her husband and son had been out duck shooting on a boat, and just as the ducks took flight and her husband started shooting, their son stood up in front of him and was shot and killed. It was a tragedy that quite understandably they had never recovered from. How could you?

The next day Keith suggested that it would be interesting

for us to visit the local TV station, so we found the place, introduced ourselves, and told them about our connection with CFCN in Calgary. The man we met showed real interest and asked us if we would like to record some songs for their music show. So we got my old guitar from the car and recorded three or four songs for them, to be broadcast some days later. Unfortunately, we didn't get the chance to see the show ourselves, as we had returned to Calgary by that time.

As we were now travelling minstrels, Keith and I went to a local McDonald's and set ourselves up to entertain the customers, which was a lot of fun. It was a great trip for us as free and easy wanderers. We stayed in Saskatoon for a few more days just exploring and enjoying ourselves, while Keith was able to reconnect with his aunt. It was a change of scene for us which is always a good thing, but then we got back on the road for the long drive through the night back to Calgary. Interestingly, I spoke to Keith about that trip a few years ago, and he had no recollection of it at all, yet he remembers things of which I have no recollection. It's strange how memory works or doesn't. It leads me to hope that my memory has not let me down in my recollection of the rest of this tale.

The outlook certainly looked much brighter for me with the icy winter long gone, and the warm summer weather with us. But I was starting to develop nagging homesickness by then. I had the hankering to visit home once again, to see my mum and my dad and the friends that I had left behind. I wanted to share my experiences with them. I wanted to tell them of all that had happened to me in such a short time over the past year and a half. I just wanted to see them all once again. I had some decisions to make.

* * *

11

PARTING

It was the Autumn, or Fall, of 1965. I had been in Canada for a year and a half and had an amazing experience. I loved it. I had adapted to Canada and the culture, I was playing guitar with the band on TV regularly, I had friends, a job, and I had my beautiful girlfriend Gayle, and all should have been well. What more could I possibly want? But it was September and looming on my horizon was the prospect of another endurance test in the form of winter and mind-numbing cold on the prairies. I was not looking forward to that at all. And I was feeling homesick.

Although I was happy with Canada, I just felt a need to touch my home culture once more, and to see my family for a visit. If I went back to England it would mean leaving the band and leaving Gayle for a while too.

I enjoyed playing with the band at dances with a live audience and getting positive feedback from them to our music. The feedback always made a difference to our performance and enabled us to give our best, but I did not enjoy the presence of that one-eyed monster, the TV camera. I always found it disconcerting to be immersed in the music, loving it playing my bass, and then when I looked up there was that eye staring right at me again. I found it unnerving.

So, having had the time of my life in the eighteen months that I had been there, I decided to leave Canada and return to England for six months and then return on the first ship through the thawed St Lawrence River in the early spring. I told Gayle of my plans, and she seemed to understand my homesickness as she had had an experience of that herself on a trip to Manitoba to visit her mum's French Canadian family. We were still very close and the love between us remained. It would be hard, but I felt that we could survive six months apart, and then resume being together again in the early springtime. We would write to each other frequently.

I told the band of my decision, and I had chosen that time to do it when there was a pause in the broadcast of our shows. That would give them time to re-organise the band before the next season. Don Wood, the compere of our show, had a creative idea and they bought me a small tape recorder with a view to me keeping them informed of the music scene in England that they would include in the show.

When I told Auntie Grace of my plans, she was very disappointed. She was such a lover of Canada that she could not understand it at all, I suppose she thought I was giving up on Canada, which many immigrants do. I can still remember her words."Well if you haven't found what you want by now, you never will." The words cut through me and they stick with me because of her great disappointment. I genuinely was coming back to Canada, but she thought that I was giving up. Even so, she wished me well and hoped that I really would return. So, with the decision made, I booked my return trip to

Travels with an old guitar

England via the same land route that I had travelled when going to Canada. That is a long train journey from Calgary to Montreal, and another ship journey, this time on the Cunard ship "The Carmania" from Montreal to Southampton.

I made my farewells to my friends, my Canadian family, and of course to Gayle, but they were only farewells, not goodbyes.

My journey back to England was uneventful. It was just a repeat of my outward journey, without the diversion of Toronto. Once again I was very impressed with the facilities and the comfort of the ship which was another comfortable journey. Ian the Scottish waiter was not on board, so I was able to stay away from too much booze.

So after a journey of around twelve days, I arrived back in Southampton, the place where it had all started for me, and there at the dockside I was met by Dad, who had driven down from Sussex to meet me.

It was marvellous to see my dad once again, after this my first venture into the unknown. We had so much to talk about after my absence of a year and a half. I was back in England again and it felt great.

I had been slightly Canadianised by then, and so was struck with the impressions that many must feel when going to England from North America. I was seeing England through Americanised eyes. The narrow, winding roads, the smaller cars, driving on the left, the rolling green hills, those funny roundabouts. Everything looked much smaller, the exact opposite of my first impressions of Canada. It appeared to me to be such a peaceful, very green landscape, with a gentle beauty compared to the majestic landscape of Canada. Both places were beautiful but in different ways. My son Joe, many years later after a visit from Canada, described the experience as like visiting Middle Earth where the hobbits live.

Dad drove me back to Brighton where I was to stay once more with Mum, so after a pleasant and thoughtful drive, I arrived back at the place where I was born and had grown up. It all seemed a bit strange and foreign to me at first, but it was just as good as I had expected. I knew it well but I had seen another side of life. It was marvellous to see my family, and friends again. That's what it was really about. I had come home to my family. My brother Ronn had returned from Singapore with a wife so it was wonderful to reconnect with him. Daphne and I took to each other from the first. Mum had re-married Rudolph, a Polish man so I went to live with them in their large flat where they had a spare bedroom.

I linked up with my old pals in the band I had played with before my wandering had begun and re-joined them purely for the fun of playing music together. After my recent experience with the band in Canada, and dealing with those awful TV cameras, I just wanted to jam with my old friends and that's all. I had had my small taste of fame on a very minor stage and wanted no more of it, and anyway, this was just a passing visit. I was going back to Canada. My friends told me that I had acquired a slight Canadian accent, which I hadn't realised, but which I suppose was inevitable.

Mum was always the sort of person to try her hand at anything. She was a very strong character and had a 'can do' attitude all of her life. I had come back to England with a box of "Chef Boy-ar-dee" do-it-yourself pizza-making kit. Pizza was still virtually unknown in Brighton but I was in love with it by then. Well, Mum said to herself, "I can do that." So she made me a pizza herself from scratch. It was awful. Poor mum, it was terrible, but she had tried.

I needed to find a job, and those were the days when jobs were ten-a-penny, so it was not hard to find something to do to earn some money. Although I still did not have a wide range of skills, I got a job selling wines, spirits, beers, and liquor at an 'off license' shop on Western Road, one of the main shopping streets in Brighton. In those days before decimalisation, the old money was in pounds, shillings, and pence, which was a very convoluted system, meaning that to sell across the counter you had to be a pretty good mathematician.

Life for me soon settled into that same old routine of work, home, eat, socialise, and sleep followed the next day by a repeat performance. And so the weeks and months rolled on. I suppose that is normal life for most of us, but it was just the sort of life that I found so tedious and always made me get itchy feet and want to move on. It was pleasant enough but I started to look towards the springtime when I could take off again when I would be free once more, unencumbered, and to feel the excitement that always drove me on.

Gayle and I wrote to each other all the time, with messages of love. We told each other about our lives, usually three or four times a week, but sometimes several times a day. There was great love between us and it gave me heart, as I looked forward to the springtime when I would see her again. I got such a lift every time that a letter from Gayle, in her beautiful elegant handwriting dropped onto the mat. Christmas came and went, the long dark gloomy days gradually lengthened and became brighter, and I booked my return passage to Canada on the "Carinthia" for the first trip of the springtime across the Atlantic.

It was March of 1966 when I said farewell to my family and friends once more and set off for Canada for the second time with a great spring in my step. I was off to the new world again. But this time, after a similar journey to the one I had made two years earlier, things would turn out very differently for me and my life would take a completely unexpected turn.

Another long journey by sea followed, and then a train journey across Canada, until some two weeks later I arrived once more in Calgary, and there to meet me at the railway station were my new friends and family. Auntie Grace, cousin Doug and my pal Terry from the band, and there too was my lovely sweet Gayle. How great it was to see her again after all those long months away. She meant more to me than anything. I felt the exhilaration once more of this new life in my new country.

We went home to Auntie Grace's house where we had a wonderful reunion party. It sure was great to be back and I was very happy indeed. So over the next couple of weeks, I set about trying to re-establish myself. I rented a small apartment of my own and set about looking for another job. All looked well. However, a gigantic earthquake was about to shake me to my foundations and hit me square between the eyes.

Travels with an old guitar

I had been back in Calgary for about 2 weeks when Gayle came around to my apartment and told me she did not want to continue in our relationship. This was the most painful, shattering thing that had ever happened to me. I was completely broken. Oblivion would have suited me. Gayle was my first love, and that love ran very deep. My cousin Ron came round to see if I was OK, which I wasn't. The tragic part of this was that Ron came to help me in my hour of need and a year later, he hit a very low point himself and committed suicide. It was such a tragedy that no one was there to give him comfort when he needed it.

Ron told me that his wife Wendy had known straight away when I had arrived at Auntie Grace's that Gayle no longer cared for me in the same way as she had done, although I had been blind to it. Girls are so good at picking up on things like that. The reasons that Gayle gave me for wanting to separate I have long since forgotten but they didn't really matter. The fact would remain unchanged. All of my plans were shot to pieces. I just couldn't imagine my life without Gayle, who had been so precious to me. It never occurred to me that anything could go wrong for us together. I was still too naive to realise that young love is a very vulnerable thing. I had been foolish to have left her for all that time. So there I was stranded high and dry.

I do believe that out of nearly all bad events in life comes something good in the end. I have found this to be true time and again in my life. And what had happened to me then changed me in many ways forever. The downside was that I vowed I would never again give my love freely without restraint. The price was too high. But on the positive side, I grew from the experience and subsequently, this changed the course of my life for the better. I would go on to have some truly wonderful experiences in life that would not have happened if Gayle had not dumped me.

So that was the end of Gayle in my life. My first love. The girl that meant so much to me. The girl whose memory I would treasure for the rest of my life. That was the end...

Or so I thought.

How could I possibly in my wildest dreams have imagined that 42 years later as I arrived by plane at Calgary airport, there waiting anxiously and nervously for me would be my still beautiful, elegant gorgeous Gayle? Waiting to greet me, embrace me, pick me up, and drive us away together to her home in Palm Springs California.

But that's another story altogether. Later.

I was in what felt like the carnage of my life, and for a few days I was lost in despair, but then my cousin Doug came to see me and told me that he was going to go and live in Vancouver on the west coast. He asked if I would like to go with him. I had no interest or incentive to remain in Calgary anymore so it seemed like a good option to me. Calgary would only be filled with sorrow and sadness. The prospect of a fresh start in Vancouver would probably be the best thing for me.

So we made plans and preparations to move on. This did not amount to much for either of us. I was already accustomed to moving, and Doug had been planning to go for some time, so within a week, Auntie Grace took us to the Canadian Pacific railway station where we set off on the train for the coast, with a suitcase each, a guitar, and a mountain of hope. It was farewell to Calgary. I was very glad to see it disappear behind us from the back of the train as we headed once more toward the Rockies and beyond.

So that was how my life had evolved for the first two years of my time in Canada, from my first thoughts of going there to the time of my stepping off the ship for the first time in Montreal, and a lot of the things that subsequently happened to me while I was in Calgary.

I have some great memories of those times playing in the band with my friends, and all those great moments of discovery in the new land. They had been exciting times for me. And, of course, those wonderful times of love with Gayle.

Setting off with Cousin Doug on the train for Vancouver marked the beginning of another new life for me, full of life's adventures, and discoveries. My roaming led me on to have some more interesting experiences, some good, some not so good, over the next few years, and that gives me a good enough reason to carry on with this tale.

PART 2

* * *

12

VANCOUVER

So began my new life.

My trip to Canada had been full of surprises for me. It had so far been a wonderful experience. My intention in writing about it had been that it might be of interest to my kids to read one day to see more about their Dad's earlier life, and to anybody else who might enjoy hearing about what it is to be a young immigrant.

I had abandoned Calgary when Doug and I boarded the passenger train bound for Vancouver on the west coast of British Columbia.

Calgary held a wealth of memories for me since I had arrived there two years earlier. I had done so much in such a short time and had some great times there. I had had my two minutes of small-time fame, I had fallen in love and had a wonderful time enjoying my new country. But in the end, I had some painful experiences too. Calgary had lost its appeal to me altogether, but I had grown from the experiences and learned a few things. I had changed. My parting from Gayle had hit me hard, and it affected me at a very deep level in various ways, and I should say a little more about that.

I had been quite religious until then, having been brought up with a Baptist church background from the time I had been a small boy, with a faith that I had carried with me. It had been a part of me and had given me a sense of peace as I travelled through the world. I had an invisible guardian. But this parting from Gayle affected me deeply. It is no big thing in the grand order of things, but it marked the time of the beginning of my loss of faith.

I had been shaken up and desolate in a way that I had never known before and I felt abandoned. My invisible guardian it appeared was just an illusion, something that existed only in my mind. This incident was simply the catalyst that started me questioning my core beliefs and all that I had felt secure with. It took me a while longer to lose my faith altogether, but over the next few years, as I learned more about our world and our place in it as humans, I came to quite different conclusions about religion.

I also drew into myself because of Gayle. Our intense love for each other had been another of my pillars and had given me strength and security. It was a part of my foundation and suddenly it was gone. The carpet had been pulled from beneath me. I had been naive and foolish to think that love could survive all, and I vowed that I would never give myself so freely again. Until then I had been very open with people, trusting and caring, wearing my heart on my sleeve, I suppose. But I had changed and become more insular. I pulled up the drawbridge. It was safer.

Cousin Doug and I were off seeking pastures new as we left on the train bound for Vancouver. That journey is now a tourist attraction, and the train is known as 'The Rocky Mountaineer,' but at the time of our journey, it was just an economical way to get from Calgary to Vancouver.

The train was from the same family as previous ones I had been on when crossing Canada from the East, with an observation car, the raised double-decker carriage with glass all around giving a panoramic view of the spectacular Rockies. It gave me another chance to see them up close, and they were quite magnificent. I had seen them from the road, but being on the train as it weaved through the mountains, gave wonderful views all around. Something about that sort of scenery fires us at some deep level. At least that's what it did for me, and I know that I was not alone in those feelings. The soaring pine-forest-covered mountains topped with snow, and deep valleys with roaring rivers far below, as we crossed high above on bridges, were sights to marvel at. Seeing how the train hugged narrow ledges in the mountainside, made me wonder about the construction of this line. It was some feat of engineering. The train sometimes disappeared into long tunnels as it wound its way through the mountains. It was quite spellbinding to watch as we made our way westward toward the Pacific coast.

The journey through that high country lasted for many hours and then to the last hundred miles or so on the flat plains of the 'lower mainland', where the train eventually delivered us to its final stop in Vancouver. This city was a place that I would come to know well and was where I was to have many interesting times. It was to be my base, where I would live periodically for several years of my life.

British Columbia is an astonishingly rich and beautiful land and Vancouver is a beautiful city with wonderful surroundings. Mountains to the north, many inlets of the Pacific Ocean, the wide Fraser River; a beautiful park stretching to the sea, many fine beaches, and islands to explore, and inland a broad plain stretching to the coastal mountains

We two tired, young, delayed pioneers were on the West Coast at last. We had missed the gold rush by only sixty years or so, but we were there. The train pulled into the station on Main Street, not far from the downtown area, and our first need was to find some cheap accommodation. It had to be cheap, as our financial resources would not stretch far. The rail station is just a short walk from downtown, close to Chinatown, and it is also close to the most poverty-stricken area in all of Canada at Hastings Street and Main. This is a very sad place, full of hookers, drunks, and drug addicts, and not at all the sort of place to feel safe. It was so sad to see those poor lost humans living without hope.

"Where we gonna stay then, Doug? Any great ideas?" I said.

Vancouver

We set off from the station along Main Street. We were in a pretty seedy area, but we had to make do temporarily and so settled on a hotel called 'The Cobalt,' which was about as bad as it gets. The lobby had a few no-hopers, drunks, dropouts, and hookers, and the rooms were absolutely basic, with a communal bathroom in the corridor It was dingy, drab, dark and depressing, but we had a temporary roof for the night. It was not a good start but would have to do. Doug and I were not in our element and needed to move on pretty quickly. It was just one step away from the worst of Hastings Street, so the next day after a search in the paper, we found an attic apartment to rent in the Broadway area, about a mile away from there, that was much better for our peace of mind.

Now we were truly independent. We were out on our own for the first time and would need to fend for ourselves. No more Mum or Auntie to cushion us against the pitfalls of survival in this great big world. We would need to learn how to make meals for ourselves. Porridge, spaghetti, and macaroni-and-cheese featured strongly in our diet at first but it was a start. Our culinary talents had yet to develop. Things very quickly started to improve for us though as we soon had jobs, so with a little income things began to look brighter., especially when we began to get a social life through contacts at work. Calgary and the memories that it held for me were beginning to fade from my immediate consciousness which was a good thing for me, although Gayle would never fade entirely from my memory.

Travels with an old guitar

I had managed to get a job working in the office of a steel mill since my experience was still pretty well confined to clerical work. My task there involved collecting all of the data from the previous day's production, collating it all, and feeding it into the computer which then gave me a summary of the day's output. The process now looks very archaic. The computer was a beast that lived in its own cooled room, which it occupied from floor to ceiling and it operated based on the punched cards system invented by Noah. I would have to feed this creature with data via a stack of those cards and once fed, it would consider it all over a long period and come up with a daily report, which I then passed on to the big chief. The job was very repetitive for a human and rather boring, but across the desk from me was a guy about my age also named Jim who I befriended, and through him, I gained a wide circle of new friends.

Our apartment was on the top floor of an old wooden house, with a kitchen, bathroom, living room, and bedroom. Doug had the bedroom and I had a bed in the lounge. We had all the basics that we needed and gradually settled in, learning to find our way around the town. We had no car, but the public transport system has always been very good in Vancouver, and no part of the city is inaccessible. A favourite place of mine was Stanley Park, which covers a large area in one corner of the city. It is a green oasis with spectacular mountains to the North and the wide estuary of the Fraser River all around. It is a very beautiful spot.

Then there were parties. We invited our work friends home and our social contacts and nightlife grew. Things were going well for us. Our domestic situation did not last for long, however, as Doug soon found that he was ready to move on again. He had better ambitions and did not want to waste his life away like this, in a dead-end job going nowhere, so after just a few weeks in Vancouver, he came home one day from work and said, "That's it, Jim, I've had enough. I'm going to join the Navy."

The Navy had been on his mind for a long while. I think that even back in Calgary it had been a choice for him of either Vancouver, or the Navy, so he had come very close to this decision already, and the lifestyle which was developing around him just helped him to decide on that course. He was ready to take the plunge, so he left Vancouver for a life at sea and found a new direction in life, which was much more to his liking.

Doug had only the most basic education and had dropped out of school, but he went on from there to achieve great things. After a stint in the Canadian Navy, he got into the world of banking, got a degree through sheer hard work, and secured a job as a manager. living for a while in the far north in Whitehorse in the Yukon Territory. I didn't see him again for a long time after he left Vancouver, but we have met again throughout the years from time to time. We had shared a moment or two in our lives, which I am sure he remembers as well as me. Doug had been my first close connection with a native Canadian, and being with him had taught me much about Canadian ways. I had lost my religion along the trail somewhere but Cousin Doug had found his somewhere further along his journey and it has given him great comfort for the rest of his life.

So life moves on for all of us. No sooner had Doug left than my brother Paul wrote to tell me that he had decided that he too was about to leave the cold wet shores of England and come to join me on the cold wet shores of Canada. Paul had been married in Cyprus, but the marriage had not worked out, and he also wanted a new start in life. So he flew out from England to join me in our attic apartment. From that time on, flying was the preferred method of travel and ocean liners were in decline. I had been so fortunate to have grabbed the tail end of it. Paul, like me, had the desire to seek out new worlds... To boldly go, etc... We were about to have some great times and strange adventures together. He settled into the Canadian way of life immediately and easily. He was twenty-three and I was twenty, and we were about to indulge our adventurous spirits to the full.

This is the first time that Paul has crept into my story, so a description of him would be fitting. He and I had always been very different from the start, and our personalities had always been worlds apart. Paul had acquired Dad's ability to hold an audience in telling a story, as you will hear later, and it has held him in good stead throughout his life and enabled him to get far in his business dealings. He was a leader, while I was a dreamer, with a musician's artistic leaning. As we were growing up, we had a gang of friends, and Paul was a leader among them, while I, being three years younger, was at the bottom of the pile. I was quite inhibited and lacking in confidence, but Paul was the opposite. We were just built differently and were driven by different forces and often travelled in different directions throughout our lives. But at that time, when Paul came over to join me in Canada, we had several years of great togetherness. We were a good team and had some interesting times, as you will see in the following

13

PENTICTON

This part of the story I have managed to retrieve because for the first time in my life, I kept a diary as Paul and I went along on a long hitchhiking jaunt. Then when we got back to Vancouver I wrote it all down and sent it in a letter to Mum in England. She kept it, and years later gave it back to me, so it provided a great reference for things that I would otherwise have forgotten. I have re-written it but left parts in the original letter form to Mum.

* * *

2850 Pine St,
Vancouver B.C.

Summer 1966

    Dear Ma,

    Well, quite a lot has happened since I last wrote to you. Your two wandering boys in Canada have had a good few adventures, so here's a long catch-up letter to let you know what we have been up to.

It started about 6 weeks ago when Paul made a suggestion.

"Hey Jim, how about a trip to Calgary to see the Stampede?"

"Hmmm! Great idea, but how would we get there without a car? We could catch the Greyhound if we could rustle up the fare." I was warming to the idea.

"Well, we could try hitchhiking," he said. "What do you think?"

"Hitchhike? That's around 600 miles. Well, It's a long haul but I suppose we could. It would be good to see Auntie Grace and see the Stampede again. That sounds like fun. OK Let's do it."

Paul and I were between jobs at that time so were able to take this on. It was high summer and almost July so there was a good chance that the weather would be on our side. I had seen the Stampede before, but Paul hadn't, so it would be a terrific experience for him. The atmosphere in the town for that week was electric and the temptation was too much for me, so our big trip started. We went to the "Army and Navy" store downtown where we bought two backpacks, and over the next couple of days got some things together for the trip. We packed them until they were overflowing, and of course, we also took my guitar case containing my trusty old guitar, along with a load of other stuff. We had fishing rods and reels and fishing paraphernalia, and a million other things too numerous to mention. I'm not sure how, but we managed to pack all that stuff in there, along with the guitar.

We set off and hit the road one bright morning with all of

this stuff, with a great deal of optimism and hope. We certainly would need that. It was a long way. We were seeking a bit of spice in our lives.

We were free and easy and ready for the freedom of the road. Hitchhiking is always a chancy and uncertain means of travel, as we were to find out. It depended a great deal on luck. You never knew if you were ever going to reach your destination or remain stuck on the roadside, and we did get stuck more than once. Things started well though, once we got onto the main

Penticton

Trans Canada Highway out of Vancouver. We got a series of rides taking us through Chilliwack, Hope (appropriately), on through the Allison pass, to Princeton, Keremeos, the Similkameen Valley and finally on that section of the journey to Penticton. We stopped at a place called Hedley on the way and wandered through an old gold mine where there were shining glints of metallic elements everywhere underfoot.

Penticton is a lovely place that we enjoyed so much, and where we stayed for a few days on the journeys both to and from Calgary. We had some very interesting encounters there, and It remains one of my favourite places anywhere.

We were quite ill-equipped for this trip though and hadn't thought it through very well. When we arrived in Penticton the weather was against us, and it began to rain, but we found a great place to shelter for the night, under a road bridge that entered the town from the North. We had brought no other shelter from the weather with us, so the following morning we went into town and bought a small tent, our first essential requirement, and set it up under our bridge. We had a nice secluded spot there, close to the town, so it proved to be a good base.

The town is situated in the middle of B.C. about 250 miles inland from the coast, in the middle of the Okanagan Valley. This is a long glacial valley running from North to South, inland from the coastal mountains. It is a Lakeland area, very beautiful, and a popular holiday area in the summer. Penticton has parked itself on the land that lies between two large lakes, the Okanagan Lake to the North, and Skaha Lake to the South, and between these two runs a small river. Across this river is a bridge, and under this bridge, not so very long ago, could be found a small tent, occupied by two displaced Englishmen, with a guitar case full of stuff. But you know all about that. We were hidden from sight there from the passing world, but we were not alone, for on the flat ground beside the tent, was a small corral, where lived a horse.

I went back there many years later

We became fond of this friendly old nag, who soon got used to his new neigh---bours. We fed him odd scraps, from time to time and he would eat almost anything. We christened him Alfred, so Alfred was his new name. He liked our bag of sugar, but he also tried to eat our clothes, our hair, and whatever he could get from my guitar case. It was a good spot there under the bridge, and from there we were able to explore the town and the beaches.

In the evenings there were usually a few open fires along the beaches of Skaha Lake, where we would mingle with the young people, and with the help of the guitar, we struck up some new friendships with music and song. The rain had stopped and the weather had turned warm and beautiful. We stayed there for three days, on that leg of our journey, exploring the town, having fun, and enjoying the holiday atmosphere of the place.

We decided, after those few days of enjoying Penticton that if we were going to get to the Stampede in Calgary in time we should hit the road once more.

The Okanagan Valley is a most beautiful place with many fruit orchards. Paul and I warmed to the place with the hills all around and a series of lakes and valleys carved out by the last ice age, but it was time to hit the road again, so on we went. We packed up the tent, our backpacks, and the trusty guitar case and set off once more to the open road.

The first lift that we got took us as far as Summerland, a small town just out of Penticton, but from that point, we didn't have much luck for a long time in getting a lift so we started walking. We walked and walked. The weather was sunny and very hot. Up and up and up we went until we were far above the lake. On that part of the road, there was nowhere for cars to stop, so our only option was to just keep going. Much later, after a very long uphill hike, we reached the top of that great climb, and there to our great relief was a fruit stand where we were able to recover from the great trek from the lake with some refreshments.

Travels with an old guitar

The much-needed rest and sustenance from fruit and drinks revived us, so we pressed on and the next ride took us as far as Kelowna, another lovely town at the Northern end of Okanagan Lake. I should mention here that Okanagan Lake has its version of 'the Loch Ness Monster' called 'Ogopogo' We never saw it which won't surprise you. One unusual feature as you approach Kelowna is a floating road bridge that you cross as you enter the town from the South. We pressed right on through Kelowna and the next ride that we picked up took us on to a very small town called Oyama, yet another superb place set between Woods Lake and Kalamalka Lake, an Indian name meaning 'The Lake Of Many Colours. The Okanagan Valley was constantly presenting us with more beautiful places.

Oyama, though beautiful, was very small with just a general store, restaurant, and a few houses. There was nothing much there, but the surroundings were lovely and it was a peaceful little place. By the time we reached there, it was late afternoon, so we decided that it would be a good place to call a halt to our travelling for the day, an ideal place for an overnight stop, so we had some food in the little cafe, hid our stuff in some bushes, and went down to the little jetty on the lakeside to try our hand at fishing.

This was our first attempt at fishing in Canada and it was very successful. We had been fishing many times in England with Dad who used to rouse us at some unearthly hour, as he said that that was when the fish had their breakfast, and who were we to argue with Dad who knew everything? Never mind that we were barely conscious at that time of the day. But there we were fishing on the other side of the world in Oyama. We started getting bites right away and caught a lot of small fish, and then I had a huge bite. I had a monster on the end of my line. Maybe Ogopogo? who knows.

My little fishing rod was pulling every which way and bent double as I tried to keep a hold of the fish. I was standing on a small raft that was tied to the end of the jetty, with my feet partly submerged as the battle continued and pretty soon, we gathered an audience of passers-by. This little drama went on for a good ten minutes while I fought with the line, trying not to lose the fish until at last it began to tire and I was able to bring him closer. He was too heavy for me to lift out of the water with my little rod but I was able to bring him to my submerged feet and then walk backwards on the raft and so tip it and leave him high and dry to get him out of the water. I had caught a good-sized rainbow trout. I had never caught a fish so big and Dad would have been very impressed. It was a great moment, but we didn't have the facility to cook it, so we just freed him from the hook and settled him back into the water to live another day.

By the time this had all finished, it was getting dark so we went back along the lakeshore, where we settled down on the sandy beach in our sleeping bags for the night. There was no need for a tent. It was a lovely warm peaceful summer night with a billion stars in view. I don't think that I had ever seen so many stars. It was an amazing sight. We were far away from any city lights so the sky was spectacular, and right across the middle, the wide strip of the 'Milky Way'. We also saw several satellites tracking across the sky.

All was quiet and peaceful, and we drifted away. In the

distance on the far side of the lake, a train hooted, but otherwise, peace reigned. It was lovely lying there under the incredible array of stars, rarely seen in the City. Very gradually though, the distant rumble increased in volume, getting louder and louder, until there was a thunderous noise all around us. It sounded as though we were about to be annihilated. It was the train, and the horn was blasting, bells were ringing the wheels were rumbling, and all hell had broken loose all around us and above us. In the darkness, we had bedded down within four feet of the railway line. After what seemed an eternity, for Canadian trains are after all about a hundred miles long, this bedlam of noise and clanking and rattling gradually faded away into the distance until at last all was peace and the serene quiet under the stars returned once more.

"Are you awake?" I asked. I won't tell you what he replied.

The next morning we woke up to another warm day with clear blue skies. The weather was in our favour. We had found ourselves in a very beautiful place in Oyama so we decided to stay awhile and fish some more. It was very relaxing, so we set ourselves up again on the little wooden jetty. and very soon, Paul got a bite and caught what looked like the very same fish, or if it wasn't him, it was his brother. The same difficult process of landing it ensued, but Paul got it landed in the same way as I had done the night before, landing it at his feet on the raft.

Oyama - Just beyond the train is where we slept.

Oyama was just a short interlude in our trip but it was quite memorable for us for the peaceful time we had there. Peaceful that is except for the train. I don't think that either of us had had such good fishing anywhere before and in such picturesque, lovely surroundings. We packed our bags once more and trusted good fortune, with a raised thumb to see us on our way.

The next town that we came to was Vernon, and after that, a rather strange ride took us to a place called Grindrod. The driver and his mate were cowboys. There were two saddles in the back of the car, along with a lot of riding gear as they were on a circuit of the rodeos, travelling from town to town trying to make enough money to survive. They were both stoned. It was a strange episode, as one of them spent most of the journey slowly dissecting a hamburger. There was a small cat in the car that he kept pushing into the back with us. We asked them where the cat had come from and they said they had no idea. It was pretty strange, but that's the way it goes when you hitchhike.

We got another ride after this one, which took us to Sicamous, which put us back onto the main Trans Canada Highway and that stood us in better shape to pick up a ride. The driver even bought us a coffee when we got there. Our next ride took us to Revelstoke where it was raining again, and time for another overnight stop. We had our little tent and found a vacant lot where we pitched for the night. By this time we had become quite efficient at making camp.

The following morning we were packed up and on the road quite early but though we had been hopeful by being on the Trans Canada highway again, we were completely out of luck. We waited and waited. But such are the hazards of hitchhiking, and it was five and a half hours before we got picked up. We had just about given up by that time and had decided to try our luck by separating, to meet up further along the road. Paul went on ahead of me, while I waited, and this brought success. I did get a ride and once we were underway I asked the driver if he would mind picking up my brother too, which, fortunately, he didn't mind doing.

He was a park warden in the area that we had entered, named Glacier National Park, and Mum I have to tell you that this park is a little larger than your park at home. He had our full attention as he told us about the Grizzlies, that he had encountered many times up there in the mountains. We were then in the high country right in the midst of the magnificent Rocky Mountains.

The ride that we had with him, was very interesting and informative as he told us things about the area and the wildlife as he drove. After this, we got a ride from two young guys who were driving to Ontario on the other side of Canada, so they offered to take us as far as we wanted to go and drop us in Calgary if that's what we wanted. However, we still had some time in hand and decided that we would spend the night in Banff before taking on the last small journey down into Calgary, about 90 miles away. Banff is the last town that you come to, where the Rockies end and the Prairie begins.

We found a spot to pitch our tent on the edge of town in the woods and started to get things ready. Well, Banff is famous, among other things, for its wildlife, and of course, that includes bears. Bears were very much on our minds after hearing the tales so recently from the park warden so as we were unrolling the tent, and laying out the groundsheet Paul said,

"What's that?"

"What's what ?" I replied.

"That noise."

We remained motionless, listening intently. Silence. Or was it? We looked around slowly, then without further discussion just grabbed everything and set off fast towards town, and didn't wait to find out. But...we weren't out of the woods yet, so to speak. There was a large hotel on the perimeter of Banff and alongside it, some very long grass. Ideal. We were able to pitch our little tent in this meadow and remain invisible to the passing world. Invisible to people perhaps, but not to all creatures!

We looked around the town for a while and then as the evening wore on made our way back to the tent. The night was upon us. We heard some howling from the woods nearby. Wolves we supposed but after a while, this subsided so we dozed off to sleep.

I was unaware of the next thing that happened until the following morning when I woke up and Paul told me about it. We had both gone to sleep but about two hours later he woke up to more howling, this time quite nearby. Meantime I was snoring. The howling got closer until it was very close indeed. And then it stopped right outside the tent. He then heard an animal sniffing all around the outside.

"You awake? " he said. But all he could get from me were snores. By that time you can imagine how he felt. And then to top it off the animal stuck its head through the flap of the door to the tent. Whatever it was, it saw Paul and bolted. It may have been as scared as Paul, though I doubt that. Meanwhile, I slept on in complete ignorance of the drama, and if we'd been eaten by a bear, I would have known nothing about it and you would not be receiving this letter. Paul said that it was either a wolf or a coyote, but I guess it wasn't the time for scrutiny right then, in the dark of the night. It was gone, that was the main thing,

* * *

14

RETURN TO CALGARY

Banff was our last stopping point before Calgary and another night like that one was not on the cards. We had become very proficient at getting a lot of things into a small space by then so it did not take long until we were out on the road again. There were no signs of wildlife seeking breakfast so off we went once more. You never knew what might happen on the journey, but it was an exciting life, and the feeling of moving on gave me that taste of freedom every time.

Our last ride was from a man who took us into Calgary to within ten blocks of Auntie Grace's house. We had been on the road roughing it for about two weeks, through 600 miles of hitchhiking, and with luck, we would now get a bed to sleep in, and that would be a real luxury. A pillow to lie on instead of a jacket.

I found that although just a few months earlier I had been so glad to see the back of Calgary, I enjoyed being there again. I never thought I would feel that way, after leaving the town in the circumstances I had after parting from Gayle but I had spent my first eighteen months in Canada there. It had been my home and I knew it well. I did wonder about Gayle though, and how she was, but after our traumatic parting earlier in the year I did not want to open fresh wounds by contacting her. I was still feeling pretty raw about it.

We had timed our arrival to when we thought that Auntie Grace would be home from work, and just as we expected she was delighted to see us. We had not told her we were coming, but there was never any question of whether we would be welcome. Cousin Ron came over, Cousin Doug was there and Leo so we had a grand get-together.

One of the first things I did was to get in touch with my old mate Terry from the band. He was not surprised to hear from me at all as he guessed that I might come to the stampede, so he was pleased to come over to join the party. I phoned a few other people that I knew and a couple of days later a girl singer from another band called together some of my old musician friends and we had a grand gathering. I felt very welcome and it was marvellous to see all those old friends again.

The morning after Paul and I had arrived in Calgary a tribe of Scottish people, good friends of Auntie Grace, arrived from Castlegar B.C. so we were a rather large household by then. Somehow Auntie Grace accommodated John and his family and us though and we all had somewhere to sleep.

I described previously how on Saturday, at the beginning of the festivities, they have a pre-stampede breakfast downtown where the streets are closed to traffic and chuck wagons are set up to cook and give out free breakfasts. The T.V. stations are all there, doing outside broadcasts of the event and while we wandered around amongst the festivities, I spotted the compere of our old T.V. show, Don, so we stopped and I had a chat with him when he came off stage. I asked him about Keith, who I had lost touch with and he told me that he had gone to England.

Monday is the day when the stampede gets underway with the big parade. This is such a popular event that we had to get up very early to drive downtown and get a good spot in one of the elevated parking lots. Grace knew the best way to deal with this as she had done so every year. We had to fight our way in but we got a great spot with a fabulous view of the parade. And what a parade it was. I had seen plenty of parades before but this was one to beat all. The invited celebrity to open the show that year was Senator Robert Kennedy, with his wife beside him in an open-top car, waving to the crowd as they passed. Among the others, we also saw Burl Ives, the singer, James Drury, an actor in "The Virginian", and Debbie Reynolds. These were just some that we recognised.

There were many floats in the parade with beauty queens, clowns, and Mounties on their horses, buffalo, cattle, horses, and Indians dressed in their finery, chuck wagons, and cowboys by the ton. Each day that we were there we went to the Stampede grounds where I had been playing with my band just the year before. We saw some good shows and went to the rodeo itself, which was the heart of the stampede, where we saw bronco riding by brave or foolish men, depending on your point of view, and steer roping, chuck-wagon races, and the whole business of cowboy life. We were enthralled.

In the stampede grounds, there again was the fairground,

with all of those crazy rides that either excite you or make you throw up, and of course those freak shows. Paul had never seen these things before and was as fascinated as I was by the Indian Village, where the local tribes had come into town once more to set up their tepees where they were showing displays of their dances.

One day while we were wandering around, somebody stepped in front of me, and to my surprise, I had run into Gayle's mum and dad, Phil and Jeanette. It was a pleasant surprise to see them again. Despite all that had gone before, I was very fond of them. Her mum gave me a big hug and asked how we both were. They knew that we were in town as they had spotted us on T.V. at the pre-stampede breakfast. I asked about Gayle and they told me that she had phoned me that morning at Auntie Grace's but had got no reply. She had wanted me to come out to the house but that might have been a difficult meeting for me, so I did not want to pursue it. No need to open old wounds.

So, Mum, that was our time in Calgary at the stampede. We had a fantastic time there with Auntie Grace., I met up with old friends and we had lots of fun.

"Well, brother," says he, " I guess we've done this town."

"Yup, pardner. I guess so," says I. "Time to head on back and see what else awaits us."

So we made our farewells to the family and got back on the road again for our long trip back to Vancouver.

* * *

We didn't have to wait long for our first ride which took us up into the Rockies again, to an intersection just past Banff, where we diverged from our previous route and started South. The reason for this was that Auntie Grace's friends from Scotland had invited us to call in and see them in Castlegar on our way home. The route took us through Radium Hot Springs and Windermere, and it was on this part of the trip that we caught our first sight of a bear. A car had stopped in front of us as a bear had come ambling out of the forest and sat himself down in the middle of the road as they sometimes do. The people in the car were feeding him through the window, which is not a good idea and is very much discouraged. It was a medium-sized black bear, and certainly big enough to finish you off with just one swipe of his paw.

We saw a lot of native wildlife on our journey at different times including deer, a bull moose drinking from the river, mountain goats, and this black bear. We saw no grizzlies as they live higher up in the mountains. The bears generally do not want to meet you so if you walk in the forest they advise you to sing or make plenty of noise or wear little bells. If you find bear poo and it contains berries it's a brown bear. If it has little bells in it, it's a grizzly.

Throughout our journey, we met all sorts of people who stopped to give us a ride, which is the upside of hitchhiking in that you encounter some interesting people and dip briefly into their lives. Mostly they were normal, friendly people, but there were a handful of very strange types too. At times we were in danger from crazy and drunk drivers, and there were times when we thought that we wouldn't get through it alive. It was all down to experience and interesting though. Travelling as we were was full of uncertainty and each day brought us something different. Most of the time the drivers were interested in us and where we came from and they gave us stories of their own lives. We had many good encounters and many laughs on the trip. The people that we met were generally very pleasant.

So back to the journey. Towards the end of the day, we reached a campsite in a place called Wasa. We pitched our tent, ate some food and brewed a cup of tea. (I forgot to mention that we had a very small cooker with us among all the other stuff we were carrying). We played some music with the guitar as we did in most places that we stopped, and then slept. This area was close to where I had met the Indians when I first arrived in Canada and where the warden had taken me in for the night with his family.

The next day we pushed on South and passed through a lot of small towns getting several rides about which I remember very little, except for the one from Nelson to Castlegar. I remember that one as it was one of those times when we doubted that we were going to make it. A man in an old car picked us up. He was only going a short distance, but he drove on past there and took us the whole distance to Castlegar as he had nothing else to do. He seemed to be in a bit of a daze and after a few miles, he turned to us both, sitting in the back, and said " Would you object to a drink? "

"No, not at all," said Paul. And on hearing this he produced the bottle of vodka, that he had been hiding under his jacket, which he then handed to us in the back. He kept shoving this bottle toward us while pointing out various local places that he knew while swerving all over the road. In his daze, he seemed to keep forgetting that he was driving. He was high as a kite and we were on a high mountain road. I don't know how many times we nearly toppled off down towards the river far below. But the river didn't claim us and a while later we arrived down in the valley in the town of Castlegar. It was one of those times when we were very relieved to stop and climb out of the car. He was a nice enough guy but he nearly killed us all.

Castlegar is a town built around the logging business and at the centre of this is the sawmill, so when you arrive in the town you cannot avoid becoming aware of the most awful stink that it produces, which pervades the whole region. You can't get away from it. I suppose the people living there just become de-sensitized, but it assails you as you arrive in the town. John and his family made us very welcome and pulled out all the stops, with a big Turkey dinner in our honour. Our host, John, was a keen bagpipe player and would wake up the whole town after several whiskeys.

We stayed in Castlegar for about a week, never really adjusting to the stink from the mill but we had a good time there with John's children who were of similar ages to us and visited some of the local places with them.

We had a pleasant little diversion with this little interlude in our protracted trip, and soon we were back on the road once more. W got a couple more rides to see us on our way which were uneventful, but then there followed one from another nutter. This guy was quite drunk. The first thing that he said was,

Travels with an old guitar

"I don't usually pick up f....ing hitchhikers." We were off to a good start.

He carried on cursing for a while more, so we thought it best to just humour him. We needed the ride. He then spent the rest of the journey trying to impress us with lies that became more and more extravagant, fanciful, and unbelievable as he went on. I don't know what the point was but we just put up with it as he took us in the right direction and that's what mattered to us.

From his drop-off point, we walked the last five miles to a campsite, where we did the usual business of setting up the tent followed by a brew-up of tea. We were living quite a basic frugal existence through all of this but that didn't bother us. We were quite satisfied. It was very enjoyable and it enabled us to visit the Calgary Stampede which had been our main purpose.

It was another warm night with clear skies, a view of millions of stars and a few passing satellites. Sleeping under the stars on such a warm night was wonderful.

The next morning, once we had decamped, we pressed on to Osoyoos, at the Southern end of the Okanagan Valley, the area that we had enjoyed so much on our outward journey to Calgary. As you approach Osoyoos from the East, as we were the ground drops away for hundreds of feet to the Southernmost end of the glacial valley. The hottest temperatures in all of Canada are recorded there, due to the geography, and orchards are abundant with fruit stands on the sides of the road.

We refreshed ourselves, had some tea, and set off heading North, following the valley. We had planned to stop to pick fruit, to make a few pennies in places like this but we never quite get round to it.

From Osoyoos, we got a lift from a lady, which was a first on this trip, and quite surprising since by then we were looking pretty rough and travel-worn, and after a couple more rides we got to Penticton once more. This was possibly our favourite place for the whole trip. We intended to spend one more night there, but one night turned into a week.

15

PENTICTON II

When we arrived back in Penticton we pitched up at our spot under the bridge where our friend Alfred the horse remained in his little corral. It was starting to feel like home. Same place, same tent, same horse.

Once settled, we went to find some food, but as we were walking along the road a car stopped beside us with someone shouting "Hey Jim!" I didn't expect anybody there to know me, so it was a surprise. When they stopped I realised that it was Sandy, the first girl that I had met when I arrived in Calgary two years before when she worked as a 'car hop' at the 'A and W' drive-in restaurant. She was in Penticton on holiday with two of her friends. Things were looking up. We made a date to see them later that day when we all crowded into their car and set off for the lakeshore to join in the nightlife around the fires on the beach.

It was open party night every night during the summer with guitars and songs on the soft fine sand. It was wonderful. and we soon made some more new friends whom we were to see for the next few days and nights, and among them were a couple of guys from California, named Jay and Shives. with whom we were to have further adventures.

Penticton II

Much later that evening after most people had gone back to their homes or campsites, only Paul, Jay, Shives, and I were left, and we decided to go to a dance. It was late when we arrived. The dance was just about over and they were turning out. However, we got chatting with some girls and tried our English accents on them again which often hit a chord with the ladies. How fortunate for us, or maybe it was simply that we were different, who knows, but whatever the reason, we just made the most of it.

Now, as you know, Paul has a great way with words and does like to have fun telling stories just like our dad, so here was his chance to go to town. There was one very nice girl who came up to us when she heard our accents and asked where we were from. Paul didn't need much more of an excuse than that, and so he set forth on his tale.

" We're part of a band from England on tour."

("Oh boy", I thought, "Here we go"'.)

He said, "We're playing in Vancouver, but Jim and I thought we'd come up here to Penticton for a few days just to see the place before we start."

This had fired her interest and she wanted to know all about us but he said we couldn't tell them who we were as we didn't want any riots or trouble with the screaming kids.

I thought to myself, 'Hold on Paul, we're getting in pretty deep here' (It gets deeper!). This was at the end of our quite eventful day, so we set off to our sleeping quarters with Alfred who you know all about.

The following day was again beautiful with clear blue skies, so Paul and I made our way down to the lakeshore, and as we walked along the beach, who should we see but the girl from the previous night's encounter along with another beautiful girl. They were sisters, named Cathy and Peggy. Peggy certainly was an attractive girl and had won the title of 'Peach Queen' that year for the Peach Festival. She had been in the parade at the Calgary Stampede, so we had seen her before but didn't know it, and she was due to go to Vancouver to appear at the PNE (Pacific National Exhibition) festival. So we spent a very enjoyable day with them on the beach and arranged a date for the following night.

The sisters' curiosity had been roused by Paul's little tale and they were pressing for more information on who we were, so to keep the story alive he told them that we were part of "Joe Brown and The Bruvvers". This was almost plausible as we had the right names and had the guitar. Joe, (apparently?) was still in Vancouver with the rest of the band. I was feeling distinctly uneasy.

And so our days of partying went on. The following day we met up with our friends Jay and Shives again and this time rented a motorboat which we almost smashed up on the rocks near the far end of the lake while driving as fast as it would go. We were smashing through the waves until it almost took off, unaware of the rocks until it was almost too late. Oh! the irresponsibility of youth! This little jaunt was followed by a leisurely afternoon at the beach, swimming and sunbathing.

That evening, we had been invited to Peggy and Cathy's house for a meal, with their family, which was lovely, but it was interspersed with a lot of horrible questions. They wanted a performance, so eventually, we gave them a few old English songs which were completely out of their experience, preceded by excuses that Joe was the main singer. Paul was the drummer and I was the bass player, (in his fertile imagination). However, we managed to put on a reasonable show and somehow it all passed off.

After another night of fun at the lakeside, we retired to our hideaway under the bridge. It had all been fun so far, but things got worse in the early hours.

It was around 5.30 in the morning when I was awakened by somebody's boot kicking at me through the tent and telling us to get up. I stuck my head outside through the flap of the tent and saw that it was a policeman. I flopped back into the tent, still half asleep. Paul woke up and asked what was going on.

"There's a bloke outside....a copper," I said, then got up and went outside to be greeted by a fuming lawman.

" What did you say?" He asked.

I repeated what I had said to Paul. I didn't feel very friendly and anyway, my brain was not yet in gear. He went on to say that they didn't want us sleeping under their bridges, so we could now leave.

We had little choice in the matter, so started packing up our stuff. We had been evicted. It had been a great spot for us while it lasted but had come to an abrupt end.

It was early dawn when we left our pleasant secluded home and friend Alfred who would once more be left all on his own, with no scraps, cherries, or friendly humans to talk to him as we set off to try to find a new home. We relocated just over the hill on a piece of wasteland that was bone dry and dusty, but it served our purpose. There were lots of holes in the ground which we were later informed were the homes of rattlesnakes. It was about the hottest part of town, and the sort of dry, dusty area that they favoured, but fortunately, we didn't see or hear even one while we were there.

The following day we were inspired to build a raft.

I described before how Penticton sits on the land between two lakes, Okanagan Lake to the North, and Skaha Lake in the South, and between the two lakes runs a small river, where our recent home under the bridge had been. We had arranged to meet friends again at the lakeside, and rather than walk there, a distance of about two miles, we used our ingenuity to make a raft with the idea of drifting down the river Huckleberry Finn style.

There were some old logs, and planks of wood lying around, so we tied all of this stuff together and launched into the river. Paul tried it first. He jumped onboard with a holler and as I watched from the bank, he slowly sank completely until all that remained was his hat floating on the surface of the water. He didn't come up for quite a while and I thought that I had got rid of him at last. But come up he did, by and by, swimming for his life, trying to overcome the undercurrent which we hadn't anticipated, so this was nearly the end of his trip altogether.

We retrieved our raft before it disappeared downriver without us, but it was falling apart, so we gathered up the pieces, tied them together again, and had another go. We found that it would not support us both but with just one it would float about an inch above the water, so we took turns floating along like this with the slow current, while the other walked down the riverbank with a rope. It meant long waits sometimes for the one walking, stopping to read for a while, or just to admire the peace and tranquillity of it all.

I have to tell you that this ride on the river was quite beautiful. Not a sound from the riverbank, or the water, or the raft, just the birds singing, and absolute peace. The current would gradually turn the raft around, so that at times you were travelling sideways, sometimes backwards. As you looked down into the crystal clear water you could see fish swimming around the reeds at the bottom and then hiding when they saw the raft. We made no disturbance to the water as we drifted so that once in a while a big fish would swim right up to have a look. We received some curious stares from fishermen as we silently appeared and then disappeared drifting by. It was a truly marvellous experience.

This little episode took nearly all day as the river moved at such a leisurely pace, but eventually, we emerged into Skaha Lake to more surprised looks, and there we linked up with our American friends again. We hired another speedboat for some fast driving around the lake, this time motoring to Okanagan Falls, several miles further down the lake. It was a complete contrast to our leisurely drift down the river. Speed was never my thing and of the two I would choose that peaceful drift every time.

In the evening Paul and I linked up again with Peggy and Cathy, but our situation as part of the Joe Brown band was becoming precarious. Questions, questions, questions.

('Paul, how did you get us into this?') Questions like,

"What records have you made?" We had three or four L.P.s in England (according to Paul). We had told them that we were playing in Vancouver and they asked where? I am saying 'we,' but I'm sure you realise that 'we' means 'he'. (Help. Get me out of this.) He named a suitable place so the girls were watching papers for a mention or an advertisement which of course never appeared.

We showed a suitable alarm too that no mention was in the paper. I was more alarmed than anybody. So Paul said that we should phone, Joe, in the hotel in Vancouver to find out what had happened.

I told you it gets deeper.

Now my unstoppable, impossible brother picked up the phone, dialled an imaginary number, and after suitable pauses eventually got Joe on the phone. Or so you would think. Paul was constantly being interrupted in his talk by Joe at the other end. It was all very realistic. My brother, the actor!

So the fiction went on. Apparently Alan, our manager, had fouled things up and did not make the proper arrangements for our Vancouver booking which was off. Furthermore, Joe and Alan had had a big row, and Alan had flown back to England. Joe then went on to tell Paul that we were still scheduled to play in Winnipeg, Toronto, and Montreal on the way home as arranged, 'Oh help!' What an imagination!

"Yeah Joe, we've been having a great time up here in Penticton. It's a lovely place. We're having a brilliant time.

Jim?... Yeah, he's right here, do you wanna have a chat? Here Jim, have a word with Joe." *(Bastard!)*

"Hi, Joe! Yeah, it's great. I gather the booking got screwed eh? Yeah, we are in a mess!" (More than you think, Joe.*)*

So ended that little adventure into fantasyland. I think we remained almost plausible throughout, and the truth never emerged. I must say that I did not enjoy being in Joe Brown's imaginary band but Paul ad been let loose with his storytelling, off into the realms of fantasy. I did not like the deception, it was not my style, but I suppose it was all fairly harmless. We had a great time with Peggy and Cathy though. They were two lovely girls.

We had a heap of fun in Penticton and spent many great nights playing music on the warm lakeshore under the stars and sitting around the campfires in good company. We had not intended to stay there for so long and had spent a whole week in that lovely town; it was a highlight of the whole trip for me, but it was time to move on once more.

Paul and I had been invited to join our good friend Mary from Vancouver and her family, in Vernon, a little further North in the Okanagan Valley. She was having a short holiday there and had offered us a ride back to Vancouver, so we hit the road again after calling in to say farewell to our old friend Alfred.

We had been fortunate with our hitchhiking throughout this trip and it did not take us long to reach Vernon, where Mary picked us up and took us to the place where she was staying. When we arrived we were just in time to join a large group of people in the back of a pickup truck where we bumped and trundled our way down some gravel lanes to the lakeside for a swim. By that time we were starving and our hosts provided us with a great meal followed by vast quantities of local home-grown raspberries.

We were staying at a ranch, set on several acres, with a dozen horses out at the back of the main house. The house itself was huge, so there was plenty of room for us all. Paul and I had our sleeping bags, so all we needed was a piece of open floor and there was enough of that. Our hosts were very accommodating.

The weather was still good, and after the meal, the family went out to ride the horses. They offered for Paul and me to have a go which led to another interesting episode of learning for me. I know nothing about horses, but I was quite willing to learn. It turned out that I did indeed have very much to learn

I tried to get on to my allotted horse, went right over and fell off the other side which caused much laughter all around. Not to be beaten, I tried again and this time managed to get up onto his back and grabbed the rope in front of me, which of course is the steering device and his mane. Did I say that I knew nothing about horses? I had been raised on all those cowboy films which involved lots of riding horses and it all looked pretty easy on the big screen. All was now looking fine. I was sitting properly astride him but it was a long way down. All I had to do was just get him moving.

"Come on then, let's go," I said. but he didn't move. "Woah! Hup!" I think that was horse language but it made no difference. They told me to kick him in the sides. I didn't want to do this, but I could see that was what I had to do, and sure enough, after a little kick, he started walking. All looking good. Hey, this is fine. I can do this. But another horse that was walking along with us then started running, so my horse joined him.

I nearly rolled off one side, and then the other as he sped up. I was in a precarious situation. I hung on as best I could as we got faster trying to get a sense of the horse's movements. I was soon able to pick my moment to jump off. Right or wrong it was my instinct to get off. I saw Paul in the distance laughing at all this, but when his horse also started running it was my turn to laugh.

This was a first for me with horses but I could see that it would be really fun if you mastered the art of not falling off. It's a long way down from there. We stayed with Mary and her family on the ranch for a couple more days. I never did master the art of horse riding, but maybe one day I will get to experience it again. I could see how enjoyable it would be if you weren't terrified.

Our little sojourn of wandering through B.C. was coming to an end.

So then came the long drive back to Vancouver. When we got back there we had travelled over 1500 miles and the whole trip was fantastic. It was a lot better than I can describe for you on paper but I have written the main things I can remember. I was so glad that we had decided to do it. It had brought us into some tricky situations. I had briefly been a part of Joe Brown's band, thanks to my imaginative brother and we had discovered British Columbia for ourselves and seen its magnificent beauty. We had come close to disaster on the road several times, and not been eaten by wolves or bears, enjoyed the wonders of the Calgary Stampede, met a few crazy people, and made many new friends.

B.C. is a wonderful place.

So Ma, I hope that you have enjoyed reading this, our latest adventure.

Lots of love from your two faraway boys.

Jim

* * *

16

PINE STREET

When we got back to Vancouver after our long jaunt to Penticton and the Calgary Stampede Paul and I decided that we really could do with some more space. The attic flat was quite small, so after a bit of searching, we found a roomier basement apartment to rent for fifty-five dollars a month in an older wooden house in a nice part of town further west, off-Broadway. It was owned by a nice old Irish lady named Mrs Moore, and I think that she took to us both straight away, so we secured it and moved in.

We had the basement area and she lived upstairs from us in the rest of the house. I think that she looked upon us as being quite vulnerable young men, which we probably were, or perhaps it was just her motherly instinct coming out, but for whatever reason, we were in her favour from the first. It was an adequate apartment, suited our needs perfectly, and was in a good location for us.

We had both worked intermittently throughout this time, but we had not yet settled into anything permanent, so there were several occasions when we were between jobs and were able to take on those jaunts like the trip to Calgary for a few weeks at a time. Paul worked for a while in a shop selling records and musical equipment, and I had worked in a shirt manufacturing company, but they were both fairly meaningless, dead-end jobs. Neither of us had yet found what we wanted to do. My job packing shirts at the shirt factory could have been accomplished by a robot but it paid the bills.

I always had my old guitar nearby as playing and singing were what I most loved to do, and so it has always been with me. My guitar was an old Radiotone acoustic jazz guitar that I had picked up in England. It had always travelled with me, even on camping trips back home and I wouldn't be without it. That guitar saw me through some interesting times over the years. It was bashed, scratched, and tatty, but it was just my old guitar and it produced music.

One day Paul and I wandered into a pawn shop where I was always interested in looking at musical instruments. I tried a new 'Aria' 12-string guitar and immediately fell in love with it. I had never played a 12-string before, and I was knocked out by the amazing full sound that it gave. I just had to have it but didn't have nearly enough money, so brother Paul kindly lent me the balance. I now had another guitar to join my trusty old friend from England. That guitar saw me through all sorts of great musical interludes too and I loved it.

Sadly, many of my treasured guitars got lost somewhere in my travels. I don't know where they went and cannot remember our parting but such is life, especially if you are a wanderer. We sometimes lose those things that are dear to us and we can only live with regret. The same thing happened with the hand-made bass guitar that I had custom-built in Calgary. I sold that in another foolish moment. I wonder sometimes if those guitars found a new life somewhere and if they are still alive today. I hope so. It would be so good to see them again. I have owned many acoustic guitars in my life but because of my ongoing travels from country to country, they sometimes got unavoidably orphaned. Travelling by air meant that there was always a strict limit on how much paraphernalia you could take with you. It is regretful that I can't pick them up and play them and remember all of the places that we went to together and the times that we had, but I still have the memories and memories are precious things.

We had not been living in our new apartment for very long when news came to us that our numbers were about to increase further. Our cousin Brendan had decided to come out to join us from England. Brendan's mum and our mum were very close sisters, so we had grown up seeing a lot of him, as he had lived just a five-minute walk away from our place in Brighton. He was one year younger than me, and we had got on well together as children. So a few weeks later Paul and I took a trip out to the airport, welcomed him to Canada, and brought him back to our new abode. So then we were three.

Brendan slotted in easily with us and we spent several years doing things together and all still got on well, but there was a much darker side to his character that emerged later. However, at that time when he arrived in Canada, he was just one of the crowd.

Travels with an old guitar

The Beatles were still at the top of their game in 1966 and we heard they were going to appear in Seattle Washington, a few miles south of the border. So Paul and I and a group of our friends made plans to go down there to see the show.

We had become friendly with twin sisters from the Westinghouse family, Julie and Rossy, who lived in Seattle, in a large mansion. As a part of the Westinghouse family, the girls were used to living the high life, but they were ordinary girls and were good friends of we paupers. We had spent time with them in Vancouver where they had been at school with our friend Mary.

So our small group crossed the border and drove down to Seattle to see them and then on to see The Beatles. It was a fun trip and it was good to see the girls again, but the Beatles were a big disappointment. Their music was great but the show was not at all good for a couple of reasons. Firstly, we could barely see them from our vantage point high up in the arena. What we saw were tiny little Beatles on a distant stage. In those days there were no big screens. But worse than that was the fact that we did not hear a single note of the music from the time they emerged on stage to the time they left because of the constant screaming from the girls. Why do girls do that? It was insane. It had been a waste of time for us, and for the Beatles too, other than the money they would have made.

It was soon after this show they called it a day for touring as they couldn't perform the way they wanted to and were frustrated with not being able to be heard, They did of course carry on making some amazing new experimental music in the studio with George Martin which in my opinion was their best.

The music world changed when Sgt. Pepper was released, but their days of touring had come to an end. However, we had had a good day out with our friends and had seen those tiny little Beatles.

Seattle August 1966

It was about then, in 1966 that the hippy age began. It was the psychedelic age and Vancouver was at the heart of it. San Francisco in the States and Vancouver in Canada were the centres of those changing times. There was constant traffic and cultural exchange between the two cities, and the West Coast was where 'it was all happening, man', to use the language of the day.

Vancouver has its beautiful Stanley Park close to the centre of town, occupying a large area surrounded by water and mountains, a wonderfully scenic place, and they started to hold regular musical events there called 'be-ins', a term that fitted the age perhaps. These were free concerts featuring the top bands of the time held in the open, and going on into the night. It was a terrific setting, with the sea and the mountains in the background, and we would go to these events and hear the bands from the South, and some of the local Vancouver bands, meet friends and just absorb the peaceful, hippy atmosphere.

The music was moving in a new direction once more with artists like Jimi Hendrix, Jefferson Airplane, and Janis Joplin, and one of my favourites, 'Country Joe and the Fish'. The names were getting stranger all the time. Popular music had evolved. It was no longer a three-minute regularly structured song. More frequently it was a long ramble of rhythm, wailing guitar, and incessant drumbeat, all creating a heady feeling that captured the moment, and the changing times we were living in. It was very atmospheric and colourful. We became absorbed into that newly emerging culture. We just happened to have been on the spot as that whole thing was evolving.

I became a "hippy'" and started wearing strange clothes, like embroidered Nehru jackets, beads, and moccasins, letting my hair grow longer and wrapping myself in a blanket at those be-ins. The blanket was very practical for keeping out the cold. The older generation thought we were nuts. So the culture inevitably rubbed off on me, but the 'live and let live' philosophy, which was central to that hippy perspective had been mine for all of my life anyway. After all, I had grown up in Brighton. And underlining the whole movement there was one very simple message within that culture, which was - 'peace'. It was easy for me. I had already spent most of my life in that state of mind. We truly believed we were creating a better world of unity. Perhaps it was a bit naive in the end for human nature is what it is but we believed that we were seeing a new dawn. The feeling of peace, love, and understanding surrounding those times were great ideals and it was great to feel a part of that.

During those occasions when I was not working I took full advantage of the main Vancouver public library which had such a wealth of knowledge on its shelves. My education was short on many things I was interested in. So I spent many hours there reading up on all sorts of things. One of my favourite subjects had always been Astronomy and discoveries were being made which were changing our view of the universe. There was so much to learn and I wanted to use my free time constructively to widen my knowledge.

I had not found a direction in my life that suited me and was not sure where I was going. I had occasional menial jobs, but nothing that fired me with any enthusiasm. They were just a means of making a dollar or two to survive, but I was not unhappy with my lot. I enjoyed Canada. It was a great place to be and I just let myself get swept along in hippydom and the new psychedelic age for a while.

I had brief encounters with girlfriends but they were fleeting and never very serious. I don't believe that within the hippy community many people were looking for any real permanence. We were just living for the moment. It was supposed to be the time of free love, and heaven knows I was ready, but few opportunities presented themselves to me. I still carried my self-doubt with me and that inability to come on to girls, but my guitar helped me on my way from time to time.

England by now was a long way behind me and I had no thoughts of returning there. Although we were still just scratching our way along in Canada, life was nevertheless pretty good despite the lack of those gently swaying hula girls of my dreams that had set me out on my travels in the first place. The long road ahead was as yet unwritten, full of prospects and still to be filled. Summer was coming to an end and the rains of autumn came on strong, as they do in Vancouver at that time of the year.

And so things just drifted along, each day bringing something new that interested me until another journey of discovery came my way with the bonus of a chance to escape from the endless rain.

17

CALIFORNIA

The following section of this story is another piece that I have been able to recapture for the same reason as the Calgary Stampede adventure. We took a trip down to California and Mexico during which I kept a diary and when we got back to Vancouver, I wrote a long letter to Mum about it all which she kept and gave back to me some years later. I didn't quite recognise the guy who wrote it, but it gave me the basic sequence of events.

* * *

<u>15th Nov 1966</u>

Since I had arrived in Canada two years previously, I had seen very little of the USA, except for a glimpse across the water at Niagara Falls, and a short trip to see the Beatles in Seattle, but then an opportunity arose that was too good to miss.

Rick was a new friend of ours from Vancouver, and he planned to drive down to visit his sister Margaret in San Francisco, where she was living with a guy called Moon. He asked Paul, Brendan and me if we would like to come along.

So began another journey of exploration for us into new territories. He had a Morris Oxford. A small car, but adequate for us four with our small amount of luggage.

Vancouver was cloudy and cool when we left, so the prospect of warmer conditions as we got further south was very appealing. Autumn, or fall, in Vancouver, can seem pretty bleak with plenty of rain, sometimes for weeks at a time. It took about an hour to get to the Canada/USA border, and that's where we hit our first bit of trouble. We three English had no Visas and without them, you are only allowed into the USA for a few days and as our trip was to be much longer than that, the border guards turned us away. It was not a good start. So we tried another approach. We hurtled along the highway to the next border crossing point a few miles further East where we changed our story and they let us in. Just try doing that these days.

We were in Blaine, which was the first town that we came to in Washington State, where we stopped to cash some traveller's cheques (remember those?) for American dollars, We did not stop long there and drove straight on to Bellingham, stopped briefly for refreshment, and then on to Seattle, where we booked into a cheap motel for the night.

We had a long way to go and were keen to make progress, so we left Seattle very early in the morning and hit the road.

The freeway system around Seattle is a maze of flyovers and underpasses but after a few wrong loops, we got ourselves onto the right highway and were on our way to the sunny South.

California

Our first misfortune came when we got pulled over by a police patrol car just out of Seattle for speeding, and as we were out-of-towners the cop guided us to the local judge's house where he was outside painting his fence. He abandoned the paintbrush and proceeded to issue us with a fine on the spot.

The southern sky looked promising, so we drove all day through the rest of Washington State and on into Oregon into the night as we planned to just keep driving, and get to California as quickly as possible. So while, Paul, Brendan, and I were sleeping, Rick drove, but we were woken up in a hurry sometime in the early hours when we found ourselves at a forty-five-degree angle. Rick had nearly fallen asleep and had driven off the road onto an embankment, almost turning the car over. However, we were safe and so drove on until we arrived in Northern California at around 3 a.m. in a town called Weed. As we wound down the windows we were hit by a rush of beautiful warm air. It felt wonderful. California here we come!

We needed some sustenance by then, so stopped at a cafe for breakfast, and when the waitress heard our accents she asked us if we were a musical group.

"Yes, we're Manfred Mann." from Paul. 'Oh boy. Here we go again,' I thought. My brother's fertile imagination. First, we were Joe Brown and The Bruvvers in Penticton, now we are 'Manfred Mann.'

"Oh, Manfred Mann, I've got a couple of your records." from the waitress. ('Why not try and dig us in a little deeper Paul?')

Travels with an old guitar

"Are you on tour then?" said the waitress.

"Yes. We're playing in San Francisco tomorrow night, and then on to Los Angeles the following night."

"Oh great, I'll tell my daughter. Can I have your autograph?" This brother of mine will get us locked up before long.

It was marvellous to be in California. As soon as we were out of the mountains in the North of the State, we saw palm trees. and eventually further South we picked oranges. It was a world away from our lives in England. It was glorious. This was what my dreams had been made from. There seemed to be an easy freewheeling way of living and I simply loved it. America is the land of dreams in many ways. It has given us so many great cultural things to improve our lives, and I loved being there in the thick of it. There was a sense of optimism and 'can do' feeling pervading society, which was so unlike the English 'can't do' attitude. Here was a land where you really could live out your dreams. You couldn't help but absorb some of that feeling. There is a lot more to America of course, but that was the feeling I took from the place at that time.

We kept moving south until we got to Sacramento, where we turned to the West on a wide multi-lane highway to San Francisco. We crossed the Golden Gate Bridge and arrived, at Marg and Moon's place very tired, at about 9 a.m. It had been a very long drive through the night of over a thousand miles.

Rick's sister Marg fed us again. We were always ready for a meal. Meanwhile, we got acquainted with her husband Moon. He was a painter, a very arty person, and easy to get along with and we connected right away. San Francisco is an artistic town anyway so he was in his element.

San Francisco in the 1960s was also at the heart of the new 'hippy' scene just as that psychedelic age was beginning. The phrase 'do your own thing' was common. People there had that 'live and let live' attitude and were very accepting of people's different lifestyles. It suited my state of mind.

They took us on a tour of the City, to see places like the crazily steep and winding Lombard Street, then to a hilltop where we could see across the whole expanse of the city, and then on to Fisherman's Wharf to see Alcatraz out in the bay. The San Francisco cable cars, that go up and down the near-vertical streets, while people hang on wherever they can, were fascinating. The operators would beat out complex rhythms with the bell, and sometimes when they didn't make it up the steep hills they would just go back and try again, minus one or two passengers.

One thing that struck me was the number of African American people there who seemed to be well integrated into society making up half of the population. Considering America's awful history of slavery and racial segregation it was a surprise. Here everybody seemed to be mixing without care. At least, that's how it seemed to me at the time, but of course, I was quite wrong about all of that.

We were lacking in sleep after our long night's drive, so after our tour of the city, we were happy to just lie in the sun and soak up the heat for the rest of the day. For the next few days, we just enjoyed the beaches, the atmosphere of San Francisco, and the sheer delight of being in a warm climate.

Our trip had originally been planned to just visit Marg

and Moon in San Francisco and then return home, but somewhere along the line the plan had evolved and acquired another dimension. We had decided to go even further south through Los Angeles and into Mexico.

San Francisco had been a pretty exciting place for us. One of the things that struck us immediately was the prevalence of Spanish influence in the buildings and culture there. It was very different from Canada in so many ways. We had a wonderful time there until soon it was time to move on again.

We had about 400 miles to go when we left San Francisco, heading South once more, this time aiming for the town of Santa Paula. We had plenty of time and no particular schedule. We were just freewheeling, so we stopped at several places on the way. The beaches were so beautiful, with sand and warm sea, so we took advantage of it and swam often. We drove on down past Santa Cruz and again on into the night.

It got to around 2:00 a.m. when we decided that we had better stop for refreshments at a cafe and fortunately we found one just before they closed. I told Paul then I didn't want to be a part of any band anymore. I'd had enough of that. So after feeding ourselves on that delicious 'diner' food which was usually hamburgers and chips, we drove on and found a quiet place to sleep about 20 miles further on.

We had been sleeping in our sleeping bags, which were stored in the trunk, but now we hit another problem. Rick had left the keys for the trunk of the car in the restaurant 20 miles back. Why he would keep those keys separate I don't know but he did. So we turned around and went back, but by then the restaurant was closed. All we could do was sleep in the car until morning when they opened up again. We hadn't been there long when a police car came by and the cop asked what we were doing hanging around there at night, but we managed to convince them that we were there for a good reason so when they had gone, we settled down again to try to sleep.

The night was cold, it was uncomfortable and almost impossible to sleep with the four of us in that small car, so after a restless time trying unsuccessfully to sleep, I got out to wander around. I could see Rick's keys lying on the table where he had left them. I walked around the side of the building and saw there was a window slightly open, but I was reluctant to break in, in case I was being watched. So I called my brother the burglar. I kept watch from the front, while my accomplice broke in through the window. The others had got out to watch and all was quiet. Then I saw the burglar creeping through the dark into the restaurant. He looked around furtively, picked up the keys, and disappeared, back to his break-in window. Success. We all got back into the car and were away from there in a hurry.

We took off, now, accomplished burglars. I dread to think of how this might have turned out. We must have been crazy. The consequences of being caught were horrendous. We drove on, found a good, quiet place to sleep by the roadside and so ended another interesting day.

The reason we were aiming for Santa Paula is that it was the hometown of Shives, the guy that Paul and I had met on our hitchhiking trip through Penticton earlier in the year. After a bit of searching, we located the very man. He was surprised and pleased to see us and we had a good catch-up on the grand times that we'd had in Penticton. He was staying with a friend of his, also named Rick who welcomed us in to stay there too. This could get confusing.

Rick's place was very spacious and lovely, and here we were able to pick oranges, which was a marvel for us people from the cold North. That was a pretty special and exotic thing to me. At last, I was in the right climate that I had been seeking. They had a colour TV which was an incredible thing to us at that time when they were unknown in Canada or England. Later in the day we also met up with some girls who were friends of Shives and Rick 2. The word was out that some Englishmen were in town.

We wandering Brits had landed ourselves in the lap of luxury. We were in the warm sunshine, with palm trees all around, staying in a beautiful house, swimming in the warm sea, accompanied by lovely Californian girls. How good can it get? I don't think it gets much better.

Shives took us to the nearby Oxnard beach, where we Brightonians tried our luck at surfing, more or less without success. It was a very skilful process that we never quite mastered. Trying to get on top of the wave, and then standing up was harder than it looked. We indulged ourselves in all this luxury in these wonderful surroundings for a few more days and then left for Mexico with Shives, who had decided to come along with us on our journey South across the border.

We passed straight through Los Angeles, intending to see it on the way back, and pressed on to San Diego, right on the border. We had heard stories and received warnings about

Mexico and were told not to attempt to smuggle anything back into the USA as the consequences could be considerable. Also not to fall foul of the law while in Mexico, otherwise you might get thrown into jail and forgotten. We were mindful of these things as we got closer to the border, and before venturing into that danger zone went to the USA immigration department to confirm that we British had no visas and asked if we would be allowed back into the USA and not get stranded in Mexico. We were assured that we would have no problem, so on we went.

18

MEXICO

Border crossings can sometimes be an ordeal, so we anticipated the worst, but when we got to the Mexican side, all we were confronted with was one sleepy guy sitting there who just waved us through without any interest in seeing papers, or passports, so in no time at all, we were in.

The border town on the Mexican side is Tijuana and the contrast in crossing that half-mile from the USA is shocking. We had suddenly gone back decades from ultra-modern California to a former age. We had heard about how bad the roads are down there so stopped to get some car insurance at a place that was advertising ' car insurance, marriages, divorces.' This was not an unusual thing down there. All the small businesses seem to get into anything that will make them a dollar.

So on we went into Tijuana, which had the reputation of being a pretty rough place, and as it was then about 1 a.m., we wanted to keep as low a profile as possible and stay in the car. We drove on with the windows closed and the doors locked.

The cars that we saw were ancient and the houses and shops looked quite run down. We didn't want to sleep anywhere around there, so went straight through the town on the road heading further south towards Ensenada until we found a suitable spot by the roadside to park up.

The road itself was bad with a lot of potholes and no lighting at all, so you had to be very careful driving, but the place where we had stopped was ideal, right on the cliff-top looking over the sea. It was warm even in the middle of the night so we just slept in our sleeping bags around the car, and for the first time in a while, we got a really good night's sleep.

The following morning we drove the last few miles into the town of Ensenada, which would be as far South as we would get on that trip. It was a fascinating little town, not nearly as commercial or as scary as Tijuana, and to us, it was real Mexico.

We needed to get something to eat, but had been warned not to go near the water for drinking as most people who went down there caught the dreaded 'Montezuma's revenge' or 'the runs' so we stuck to beer. The food though was wonderful, and so tempting, even from the vendors in their little roadside stalls. I don't know what half of the stuff was that we ate but it sure was tasty. The Mexicans knew how to make things appetising, and we were able to eat plenty for a dollar.

The bars are open all day so we went in one to try the beer, or maybe tequila and were soon assailed by Mexican guitar music by three guys in enormous Mexican hats who followed us in. One of them started singing about an inch from Paul's ear. He sidled up and said,

"Hey, Pedro. You wanna song? One dollar." We weren't very good customers so they wandered back outside.

Every bar that we went into had girls who would get up

as soon as we entered and start dancing naked while propositioning us. I suppose most of the Gringos that they saw coming down from The USA were looking for just that sort of action but I wasn't. Ten minutes later the musicians came back, and the same guy came up and said,

"Nice song Amigo? One dollar." While we were there half a dozen other wandering minstrels came in plying their trade. One dollar or ten dollars seemed to be the going rate for lots of things.

I had a memorable little experience then which has stayed with me ever since. The others had gone into a shop to look around, but I wasn't much interested in shopping, so I waited outside and, lost in thought, sat on the curbside contemplating Mexico, sunshine, 'life, the universe and everything'.

I hadn't been there long when a scruffy little boy of about ten came along and sat down beside me. He just sat there looking at me. I said a couple of things to him, but soon realised that he didn't speak English, so I said,

"Buenos dias, amigo." With that, I had exhausted my knowledge of Spanish.

"Buenos dias," he replied, and that was it. We just looked at each other for a while. We had run out of any means of conversation. I started humming and singing quietly to myself, whereupon he picked up a rusty old piece of pipe that was lying in the gutter and started blowing into it making musical trumpet noises to go along with my singing. We carried on like this for a long time together, stopping occasionally to just smile. We had somehow connected and were, communicating

166

just through music and gesture. Neither of us could speak to the other but we had found a way to interact and overcome the language barrier. To me, it was a magical moment that I have never forgotten. Then his mother appeared and hailed him from across the street and off he went.

It's worth repeating that the street food was amazing. We were taking a chance to eat food from those wagons parked by the side of the road, but the smells were so enticing. It was fantastic and I couldn't get enough of it. Who knows what they did to the food but it was worth the risk for the amazing flavours.

Ensenada was great, but after spending another day there it was time to head back North, so we left town and found another place on the roadside to sleep away the beautiful warm night. Shives was already surfing when we woke up, so we went down to the sea to join him. What a great time. Surfing in the warm sea in Mexico. It was pretty damn good.

We got back on the road once more and headed back to Tijuana, this time in daylight where another scary event awaited.

Tijuana is commercially aimed directly at the American tourists who come across the border looking for girls, drugs, cheap goods, or whatever else, and consequently, people are trying to grab you in the street all the time, trying to sell you something. As we walked along the street the taxi drivers would shout,

"Hey, Pedro. You want some drugs - cheap?"

"No thanks."

"French movies? One dollar." And so it went on. Guys would come up and say,

"Hey, Amigo, you want nice girl? My Seester. Ten Dollar."

We walked on a little further and another shady character sidled up to us and said something similar.

"Pssst. Hey Meester. You want nice young girls? Ten dollar. You come see. No like it, no take it."

So being somewhat amused, and perhaps somewhat stupid, we followed him to see what would happen. He led us to an old building, which you might call a 'house of ladies', or you might have some other name for it. A strong smell of disinfectant assailed us. This had gone too far for my liking and Rick had already bailed out.

We found ourselves at the foot of a wide staircase with a lot of girls leaning over the balcony above us. Shives was the only one who was interested in being there. The rest of us were just tagging along which is why we had come that far with him. We climbed the stairs, God knows why, and when we got to the top, a girl grabbed each one of us and dragged us away, each into a different room.

Now I was a lusty 20-year-old, but I was not ready to chance anything with a lady of her profession in such a place. "Oh Boy." I thought. "How the hell to get out of this one?" I said to the girl as I tapped my pockets,

"Oh. I've got no money. I'll just have to go and see my brother," she said,

"It's ok. You no like me? I get another girl."

"No no, it's not that." I didn't want to offend the poor

thing. And with that, I went out into the hallway in time to see all the others doing the same. We ran. All of us except Shives, that is, who stayed for the show. I was not likely to forget that experience in a hurry.

Then we had to search for Rick in this dangerous city and couldn't find him anywhere. We went into several bars, where the girls kept trying "Ten dollar?" but no Rick. All the bars were the same. I was walking along in one of them looking for Rick when a voice came from a dark unlit corner saying,

"Hey, Glasses. Ten dollar?" There were men in the streets trying to sell women, watches, rings, and lots of trash. Most things seemed to be ten dollars. We grabbed some more food, but there was still no sign of Rick. We had wanted to get clear of Tijuana before nightfall, but we couldn't leave without him, and it was getting dark. We just had to hunt him down. We found the car, but no Rick. We split up and carried on searching, and at last, Paul located him, along with Shives, who had reappeared smiling and happy. And with that, we made it straight for the border, and back into the USA. We had no difficulty crossing and were back in the modern world once more. There were a lot of Americans also returning, looking worse for wear after their binge in the land of Tequila.

Mexico gave us one hell of an experience, and I wonder why we put ourselves into those situations, but still, I am glad that we did. At least we learned a bit more about this big world around us.

It was Friday night and we drove straight through San Diego, past Disneyland, and into Hollywood and Sunset Strip, where we parked up and had a walk around to take it all in. The place was hopping. Any night was a fun night on Sunset Strip after dark, especially on a Friday. As the evening wore on, we went into a cafe to have a drink and plan our next move. Rick, Paul, and Shives wanted to press on back to Santa Paula, but Brendan and I were keen to have a look around Hollywood, so the two of us decided to stay and take our chances.

The others continued North while Brendan and I set off into the unknown of Los Angeles and Hollywood. We were alone in the big city but ready to just go with the flow and see what might happen. We were as carefree as ever but we seemed to have been blessed with good luck many times on this trip and we hadn't gone very far when we fell in with a group of people who, when they heard our strange accents, asked where we were from and where we were going.

They offered for us to stay at their place for the night, so we joined them for the rest of the evening. But when we got back to the house Brendan and I found that we had a problem. Mexico had caught up with us in the form of what was commonly called Montezuma's revenge. We had avoided drinking the water down there but the bug had still got into us, probably from the food, so when we got to the house we spent the rest of the night racing each other to the bathroom every few minutes. It was not very pleasant. Fortunately, the bug did not last long and I could never regret eating that wonderful Mexican street food.

We had an aunt living in L.A. named Auntie Bunty, married to Bosco, who was another artist, so we wanted to make contact while we were in the area and phoned her. We had met her once or twice in England. She was very glad to hear from us, and so we made our way down to her place somewhere in Southern L.A. where we found great hospitality once more. First of all, she fed us, as all aunts seem to do, then she gave us a beer each which we consumed in the garden sitting in the sun before taking the opportunity to use the shower to make ourselves a bit more presentable. She was most interested to hear about the family in England, which Brendan was able to update her with as he had been there most recently.

On Saturday night, Auntie Bunty drove us back to Hollywood and invited us to come back later to spend the night, so we were then free to explore and take in the highlights of Sunset Strip.

Life is sometimes filled with strange coincidences and here comes one now.

Back home in Brighton when I was playing in the band with Pete, there were many other groups apart from ours on the music scene and one of these was "Bobby Sansom and the Giants." So as Brendan and I walked along The Strip we saw a poster on a lamppost for a place called the Hollywood-a-go-go, and the advert read, - "Direct from Brighton, England, Bobby Sansom."

The venue was close by so we went straight there and after speaking with the doorman, we got Bobby out to meet us. We had never actually met in Brighton, but he knew of me and I knew of him. We talked about old times back home, and all the other groups that we both knew. He repeated what I had already found for myself, namely that it was an advantage being English in music at that time in America. He was going up in the world and doing well making a living as a singer in Hollywood. He looked every part the professional performer, dressed in a flamboyant jacket with immaculate hair. He was able to carry it off well and deserved his success.

Brendan and I went on from there to a cafe and as we sat we wondered how we were going to get back to Auntie Bunty's. Brendan, unlike me, was good at chatting up girls so we chatted with a couple of girls, using our very best English accents, and they kindly offered to give us a ride there. Their names were Mary-Ellen and Gail, and it all went splendidly. They were interested in us and where we came from, so before we left them we made a date for the following day, where they offered to drive us around Beverley Hills and other places of interest.

It was late when we got back to Bunty's place so we crept in quietly and off to bed. The following morning, after a good breakfast with our hosts we got picked up by the girls and went for a drive around Beverley Hills, where they pointed out some of the houses or more accurately, mansions, of the famous movie stars and told us who owned them.

Disneyland was our next call which was a marvellous experience for us. We saw all of those attractions of Fantasy Land, Frontier Land, Tom Sawyer's Island, and all those good things about the history of the USA. These were all accessed from a nineteenth-century style Main Street, a touch of old Boston, with gunfights among cowboys every hour or so. Walt Disney created a wonderful place where imagination was brought to life. We had a lovely day there with Mary-Ellen and

Gail and at the end of it all, they took us home to Bunty's. We arranged to see them again the following day. Well wouldn't you?

The morning brought another beautiful warm sunny day as seemed to be normal there, but to us, every such day was a treat. Our lovely hosts took us to Laguna Beach, a wonderful place, with soft sand, palm trees, and the warm Pacific Ocean. I believe that we were in paradise with such company. We had taken some beer down there with us and a little later a Land Rover drove up to where we were and out stepped two policemen. We got a small telling-off as drinking was not permitted on that beach. The drinking age was 21, which we were not, and the girls were only 18, but we managed to charm them and no charges were laid. The interested spectators on the beach got no satisfying arrests.

The girls took us back to their place to eat, and from there we phoned our amigos to arrange our pick-up. So after a while along came Rick and Paul and we said farewell to our lovely friends Mary-Ellen and Gail. It was such a pity to leave them when we were just getting to know them. We had had a couple of marvellous days with them and it would have been so easy to continue, but Brendan and I were stranded and needed our ride.

It was time to set off back to Santa Paula, where we stayed for just one more night, and the following morning, loaded up and set off for San Francisco.

It was Farewell, Santa Paula. Farewell Los Angeles. Farewell Hollywood. Farewell Disneyland. Farewell Mary-Ellen. Farewell Gail. Farewell wonderful Southern California.

Travels with an old guitar

Yes, I would rather have stayed.

Soon San Francisco appeared before us before long and it was on to Marg and Moon's to sleep. After just one night in their good company, we set off driving north as far as Redding in Northern California where we stopped for the night while we were still South of the mountains. It would be warmer there than beyond.

We found a suitable spot and set ourselves up as usual in sleeping bags, in and around the car, and as conversation faded by degrees, gradually the quiet of night came down upon us. It was another glorious night of a million stars. Peace. Then --- in the distance, ---a train, which got louder and louder, until it passed us, a-bangin' and a-clangin'. within about ten yards of where we lay. I would not have believed that this same scenario could happen to Paul and me a second time, but it did. There once again was a railway line, just a few yards away from where we lay, and another damned train tearing through the night and our tranquillity.

The following morning we went back to the cafe where we had previously been "Manfred Mann". I was apprehensive of probing questions, but fortunately, there were different staff working that morning so no embarrassing questions, just a good breakfast feed. We drove right through on our return journey, past the Northern California mountains, on into Oregon and Washington, across the border and on to Vancouver. The further North we got, the colder and darker it became, and when we climbed out of the car at the USA /Canada border, we nearly froze to death. It felt like Iceland. We drove into Vancouver in thick fog and arrived home at about 2:00 a.m. We were back in Canada. And that was it. That was the end of our little adventure to the warm Southern lands.

What an amazing time I had experienced. I had tasted paradise.

All that time ago when I started to travel from my home in England those were the sort of places that I had been seeking. The trip through California and Mexico was filled with wonderful memories for me, but it would not be the last time I went South.

19

HOUSEBOAT

After living in Vancouver for a few months we had developed a large circle of friends, some of whom came in search of a place to stay, so over the following weeks, and then months, one by one, two by two, or three by three, the numbers grew in our basement flat on Pine Street until the floors were strewn with bodies in sleeping bags every night. The word was out, and our place had become a refuge for wanderers. Some were migrating to the coast from the interior of B.C., some from thousands of miles away in the East of Canada, and some were draft dodgers from South of the border just trying to avoid having themselves blown to pieces in Vietnam. Who could blame them for that? What our landlady, Mrs Moore thought of this I'm not sure. We wouldn't let her in.

I remember one of our many new guests by the name of Spider. Well they were strange times. Spider would sit for hours with the chessboard in front of him waiting for an opponent. Sadly we heard later that he had jumped off a bridge in Montreal.

We were constantly receiving new guests, and one day a

new arrival came with some awful for me and Paul. He was from Calgary and told us of some local news there that a guy by the name of Ron Bonsteel had committed suicide. This was our cousin Ron. It was devastating news for us, and sadly it was his mum, our Auntie Grace, who had been the one to find him in his car the next morning where he had rigged the exhaust to feed back inside.

Poor Auntie Grace. As if she hadn't been through enough turmoil in her life already. Ron had been having marital problems and this was compounded by the fact that his baby son had died by jumping through the floor of his cot. It had all got too much for him. Ron had been in trouble with the law in his earlier life but when I met him he was a lovely, kind guy and it was a tragic, sad waste of a life. If somebody had been there to help him get through that moment he would no doubt have found happiness and lived on through these past fifty years as a part of our wider family. Suicide is always such a sad, sad thing for everybody in the family. I will always remember Ron coming around to see me through my darkest hours after parting from Gayle, and how very sad it is that there was nobody there to help him through his bleakest moment.

The basement apartment had become more than I could handle, with all of those people strewn across the floor every night. It was like a refugee camp. I needed to find somewhere quieter, and Brendan felt much the same. We decided to move on and went looking for somewhere that we could rent together. We came across a houseboat, moored in Vancouver

Harbour that we could have at a nominal rent.

I had never had anything to do with boats before, and living on one meant rising and falling with the tide, and adjusting to the rolling from the swell. Everything on a boat is a bit more condensed in space, but there was enough room for the two of us, with a sleeping space each, and a small galley. It was quite a novel way to be living compared with life in an apartment and we enjoyed it. At high tide, it was a simple matter of taking one or two steps on a ladder to step onto the dock, but at low tide, it was a different matter. The ladder from the boat jetty to the dock was then about 10 feet long, mostly covered with green slime, so needless to say, we had very few visitors at those times, especially among our lady friends.

There was another slight problem with the boat in that it was sinking. There was a leak in the hull, and the bilges needed pumping out every few days with the electric pump which needed to be primed and run for an hour or two. It was a messy business, and Brendan's natural aversion to work of any kind meant that the task almost always fell on me. As the bilges filled, we would sink lower and lower into the water until we could feel the sluggishness of the movement of the boat against the swell, but Brendan would let us sink rather than operate the bilge pump.

At least we were completely free of neighbours there and it was a cheap way to live which suited us. We had a good location in the harbour surrounded by boats, big and small, some of them quite luxurious' We could look out across the water to Stanley Park, with beautiful mountains in the distance beyond.

Houseboat

Our friends enjoyed coming to see us in our nautical setting, and pretty soon we got quite accustomed to anticipating the tides. It was an interesting time which I enjoyed for a while. We had adequate heating and water and comfort of a sort and were fairly close to downtown. Fortunately, we did not experience any stormy weather while we were there. Maybe that would have put a different feel to it. We had a radio, a guitar, a chessboard, playing cards, and books and we amused ourselves with all of these and our visitors. I enjoyed the water-bound life for a few months but there came a time when I had had enough of being the bilge-man and abandoned ship for life ashore and got myself a one-room apartment in an old building in the Kitsilano area which would be my home territory for the next few years.

Brendan could either operate the bilge pump or sink as far as I was concerned. He may have been my cousin, but he was by a very long stretch the laziest person that I have ever encountered. He has rarely if ever worked and has made a career of using other people in whatever way that he could. There was worse to come, but that's probably enough said about him at this stage.

Somewhere around that time, I met some guys who became very good friends and remain so today, and one of these led to was my first experience of sailing.

These friends were from a variety of places and we all shared a European background. They hailed from Wales, Scotland, Ireland, and Holland, and had all gravitated to Vancouver. As my Irish friend Dave says, "We were a small, select bunch of misfits." I realised fairly quickly that I had all the right credentials to join them.

Paul L, as I will call him to avoid confusion with my brother Paul, was of Welsh origins. His parents owned several houses in town, and soon after we met, he became my landlord when I moved into a room in one of them. He was a keen sailor and we took many trips sailing the offshore waters around Vancouver visiting some of the smaller islands on his Trimaran.

I didn't know anything about the principles of sailing. I left that all to Captain Paul, while I sat and played my banjo, occasionally manning the tiller while Paul attended to the sails.

It was wonderful sitting there in the sun with the mountains in the background and the wind in our sails, the sound of the sea lapping against us as we gently made our way across the straits, while I just quietly played tunes. The small islands were mostly uninhabited and we would sometimes moor up and stay the night alongside other boats. You had to pay careful attention as to just where you are on the map because in that area the islands belonging to the USA and those of Canada are very close and if you put into an American island you were required to announce your presence to the border control authorities. Fortunately, Paul had good charts and was quite familiar with the area

On one of those trips, I was intrigued to see a huge eagle in a tree just a few feet above us who was clearly quite unafraid and just watched us as we passed below.

Paul was working in the newsroom of a local TV station and another hobby of his was filming. He made several short documentary films on the offshore islands about the area where we lived and some included those trips of ours.

on a later trip with Ukulele

Another of my select bunch of misfit friends was Joost and it was through him that I first came to try my hand at performing solo. It was a new venture for me that had mixed results.

Joost was originally from Holland and has lived in Canada for most of his adult life although he still retains a Dutch accent. He spent his very early life as a small boy in a Japanese prison camp in Indonesia, where he nearly starved to death living on scraps, but that is buried long ago in his past and he is a happy, jolly individual. He is an artist, a writer, and a man of many talents.

Joost had been going regularly to a folk club in town and one day he said to me,

"Jim, you should come along too. People would like what you do. Just come along and give it a go."

He kept encouraging me and after I while I agreed. I had played with bands before, playing bass guitar, and I had sung and played guitar at parties plenty of times, but I had never put myself out there like that before, singing solo in front of a real audience. So I agreed to give it a go and went along there with our little gang. I was very nervous when my turn came to get up on the stage but to my amazement Joost was right; they liked me. I got great applause and they asked me to come back the following month. It was a great morale boost and I was pleased with myself for having accomplished it. It felt very good to be appreciated like that.

So the following month I did return, again with my gang, this time feeling quite optimistic. I got up there in the first half and did much the same as I had done before but this time the reaction was quite different. The audience just ignored me and carried on talking to each other. I was devastated. I was not at all used to performing solo and had been nervous to begin with, but that finished me off. It was a learning time and I have long since learned not to be bothered by that. Sometimes people are more interested in socialising with friends than listening. Sometimes you win. Sometimes you lose.

It seems strange now to think that these sorts of events were invariably held in smoke-filled rooms, where a pervading blue haze was normal.

Houseboat

There came a pause and a refreshment break during which time I would have been happy to call it a day and go home before the second half, but I didn't. I felt committed to doing the second half and when that came around I had to somehow get up there and try again.

So this time I took my gang up with me for moral support. I had Paul, my Welsh friend, Dave, my Irish friend, Joost from Holland, Jimmy from Scotland, and Bob, the only Canadian among us up on the small stage with me. It was a folk club, but we were not confining ourselves to folk music. We had drums, bass, and electric guitars and were not at all like normal folkies. A few frowns appeared. The first song went reasonably, but from there it went downhill. I sang a few and then we moved on to do some Rolling Stones songs with Jimmy singing. It was not at all folky. I don't recall now what songs we did but what I do remember is that at the end of the evening, they asked us never to return.

Unfortunately, there is a sad part to this story of my small group of misfit friends that I should include here.

Bob, our good Canadian friend, who was very much a part of our little troupe took a trip to Europe where one day he was travelling in a car in Germany with three other people, and they turned the wrong way into a one-way system. Everybody in the car was killed except for Bob, who was very seriously injured. He spent a long time in a hospital in Germany and was later flown home to Vancouver where he made a further recovery. I met him after that and he did not remember if he had known me before his accident, or where he had known me. That was very sad for me, and I remember that he often said, "I should have died in that accident." He knew me, but could not fill in the details as his brain had been damaged in the accident. We had been great pals and had done many things together before he went to Germany. Then a few years later I was informed that Bob had killed himself. It came as a tremendous shock.

Looking back on all of this I am amazed that I was able to cram so much living into those years of 1966 and 1967. I had been working in England; then returned to Canada; parted from Gayle; and went on to Vancouver with Doug; Paul came over to join me; we hitchhiked to the Calgary Stampede; I went to Mexico; lived on the water in that houseboat and a whole lot more. It had been quite an eventful couple of years.

20

CALIFORNIA HITCHHIKING

Brendan had also abandoned the nautical life when there was no slave to pump out the bilges, so he moved into a room on the top floor at Paul's rooming house, and by degrees, as rooms became available more of our friends moved in until we effectively had the whole place to ourselves. Brendan, Bob, me, Joost and a few others each had a room and at night we would all get together with Paul, our new landlord. It was a good time for our happy little group. April came, and with it came my 21st birthday, marking three years since I had come to Canada. This called for a big party. Our house was teeming with people. I didn't know half of them but I do remember that my pals got together and bought me a present which I found very touching.

Cousin Brendan then got himself in a bit of trouble when he was busted by the narcotics department for possession of cannabis.

Unfortunately, because of that we all became tarred with the same brush as him, as a result of which we got evicted from the house by Paul's dad. Our friendship with Paul was unaffected, but who could blame his dad for this? We had a great time living there together but as George Harrison sang, 'All things must pass'. So I found myself a room in an old house nearby, still in the Kitsilano district.

My brother Paul had started to find a new direction in his life and career by that time which served him very well in the long term. He was always much more practical than me, and although he was there on the periphery of that hippy world for a while he soon left it all behind him.

He opened his own business in manufacturing and then importing cassette tapes and did very well in it. He was able to put his talents to good use and never looked back. He went on to get into the business of memorabilia and opened a shop selling many of those items online, such as photos of celebrities with signed autographs. He then got a contract with MGM to sell props from the Stargate TV series and moved on to managing a famous actor. He was also involved with a gold mining enterprise in Tanzania where he had several Canadian investors signed up. Paul was a great entrepreneur.

We had shared some great times in our lives and travels over the previous year or two which I am sure that he remembers with great fondness, and I hope that he gets to read all of this one day.

I was between jobs again, so on an impulse, I packed my bag, and with my guitar set off once more to hitchhike down to California in search of the sun.

It was illegal to hitchhike in the State of Washington, so I caught the Greyhound bus from Vancouver right through Washington State to Portland in Oregon, where hitching was legal. From there I was able to pick up a few rides that got me by degrees through Oregon and into Northern California, where I found myself once again in the town of Weed. With night coming on, it was there I got firmly stuck. I simply could not get a ride. Unlike before when I was there and it was warm, this time I was cold, wet, and miserable, and was getting more depressed by the minute. I could not see my way out of there and succumbed to the fact that I wasn't going anywhere, so made my way to the Greyhound depot where I curled up for the night, freezing while waiting for the first bus to get me out. Time slowed down to a crawl and that was a pretty low point for me

It was hard to sleep, being so cold but in the early hours, I took the first Greyhound out of there and rode the whole distance to San Francisco. I had become a bit disheartened by hitchhiking. Getting stuck in Weed had not been at all pleasant so I took the safer route. I made my way to Marg and Moon's abode where we were always welcome, but when I got there not a soul was to be found, so I went to a nearby park to await their return and this led to a very unpleasant experience.

I got chatting with a guy, who asked me about my situation, and as he lived just over the back of Moon's place. He said I could come back there and wait if I wanted to. It was a very friendly and kind offer so I took him up on it. We went back to his place where we enjoyed a beer together. From his window, we could see the back of Moon's place so I would be able to see when they got home. But as the evening wore on, they didn't show. The guy said he would be okay with me staying there for the night if need be. I didn't have a lot of options, so I agreed.

We chatted a while and had another beer and still, there was no sign of Marg or Moon. I wanted to settle down on the couch but he said I could sleep on the bed. I was reluctant to, as he was there as well, but some distance away from me. It was a big bed, but the whole thing made me very uneasy. That was not my scene! So just as I was drifting off to sleep I felt his arm come around me. I froze for a moment and then jumped out of bed. He woke up and said,

"What's up?" I told him what had happened and he said

"Oh, I'm sorry, I must have been dreaming." He was very apologetic, but I'd had enough. This time I insisted on sleeping on the couch. I wasn't going to risk it again. Gayness was not my thing.

So I slept, without incident, and in the morning he was as nice as could be. The night's incident was forgotten and he made me a big breakfast before I left. I had been naive and had not understood what I was getting into. San Francisco is known to have a large gay population and I should have known better but I came to no harm.

I went to Marg and Moon's and found them home and welcoming as always, but I didn't tell them of last night's ordeal. It was good to see them again and I stayed there for a few days enjoying the San Francisco scene once again.

It was an exciting time to be there at the dawn of the 'hippy' times. I had my guitar with me, as always, and we had some grand times singing songs with Moon using saucepans for drums. I decided to go on to L.A. again so set off once more heading South to the land of oranges, lemons, beaches, and wonderful warm sunshine. My wandering journey continued. Some hours later after good fortune and successful hitchhiking, I arrived at Auntie Bunty's place.

I had no real purpose in these travels. I was just drifting around California, meeting people and enjoying the place, soaking up the warmth, and culture. It was a good deal better than Vancouver in the rain. The main attraction for me was the endless sun and warmth. It was easy on you and very comfortable for the soul. I warmed to not only California but the whole American lifestyle and culture.

The life of drifting just suited me at that time. I would be taking in the scenes around me, and there was always a multitude of things buzzing around in my head. It was mostly a solitary time, but I was okay with that. I have always enjoyed those times of solitude, and when I encountered somebody the conversations we had were usually an interesting diversion. We are after all social creatures and after those solitary times, I always needed to return to the real world of people.

I stayed with my aunt for another night, enjoying her hospitality and company, and in the morning set off on the road once more.

I was all set up by an on-ramp to the freeway waiting on the roadside trying to get a ride out of L.A. when a police car came up to me and stopped. The cop told me it was illegal to hitch on the freeway but if I hopped in he would take me to a place where I could hitch.

Travels with an old guitar

When we got underway I found that he was very friendly, and asked me all about England. We got on brilliantly. I told him about myself and why I was there, and he reciprocated. We talked about England, the USA and lots of things. He was a nice guy and drove me about 20 miles until we were out of the freeway system where he set me down in a good spot to hitch. I was just getting out of the car, saying goodbye and 'thanks' to him when he said,

"Oh hang on, just a sec." He then wrote me a ticket for hitchhiking on the freeway. I didn't see that one coming at all.

Most of the encounters that I had in hitchhiking down there were not particularly memorable, just ordinary, people taking me a few miles in the right direction, but I do remember one person that I met.

I was on the roadside hitching alongside another guy who I got to know briefly as we waited for a ride together. He was American, aged about 20, and was going to see his girlfriend in San Francisco before flying to Vietnam with the army the following week. I have sometimes wondered what happened to him. He was a young man just like me with his life in front of him, but unlike me, he faced the possibility that he might be blown apart or maimed within weeks. We were so similar, but our futures might be very different. For all I know he might have not seen these past 50 years, I have no idea but have occasionally wondered about him.

I made it back to Moon's place in San Francisco, avoiding the park, and stayed for a day or two more. It was handy having a place to stay there as Moon was always welcoming.

I wanted to explore San Francisco some more. It was

California Hitchhiking

Hippysville Central in 1967 and I went to the centre of it all, the Haight Ashbury district. The place was full of hippy shops, beads, colour, music, and welcome smiles. There was an atmosphere like nowhere else. It was all 'Peace and Love and sharing' and was very easy to blend into. Conflicts and aggression seemed to be a million miles away. At least that was the feeling I absorbed from being there.

Hippies had congregated there from all over America. It was *the* 'happening' place. People were giving and sharing, and it felt as if we were all one big family. I guess we were a new tribe, just enjoying being together. It certainly felt as if the world had entered a new phase and San Francisco was the place to be. This is somewhat paradoxical since the Vietnam War was in full swing. and President Johnson was busy sending more and more American young men to their deaths in a hopeless war. America was a land divided.

So once again, after I'd had a few more days in San Francisco, being "Cool in my tribe man," to use the language of the day, I stuck my thumb out once more, guitar at the ready, and hit the trail again back to Vancouver.

That was my first solo hitchhiking trip South to California but over the next few months and the following year, I did it several more times when the opportunity arose. Occasionally, details come to mind about places and people that I met.

I was back in the Haight Ashbury area of San Francisco the following year and the change was enormous. That friendly open spirit had gone. There was a more sombre mood around me and the place had gone to ruin. I saw a dead dog in the gutter which people were just walking past and ignoring.

That hippy spirit had vanished to be replaced by something much darker. I think that hard drugs had taken over. I remember being in a shop there when two black guys came in, and one was saying to the other,

"Hey man, look at all these white folks. See how they stick together." He was quite aggressive. The racial problem that I had been blind to on my previous visits was still there as it always was. I thought I had seen racial integration before but I was wrong.

21

DRIFTING

My employment career was still in the doldrums so I decided to take another trip to the Okanagan, this time to pick fruit. It was another hitchhiking enterprise as I had not yet got around to driving again after crashing into the lamppost back in Calgary. Most of the time I seemed to be able to get from place to place, as long as I was prepared to wait. Sometimes I'd be stuck on the roadside for an hour or two, but most times I could get a ride sooner than that. I tried my best at those times not to look too much like a tramp to improve my chances of getting a ride. I am not sure whether the guitar that was always with me was a help or a hindrance. I like to think that it was a help but that may be right or it may be wrong.

However, this time I had success and within a few hours of leaving Vancouver, I had managed to get to Oyama again, the place where Paul and I had stopped on our trip to Calgary and had had fun catching fish from the jetty.

The Okanagan is a centre for fruit growing with many fruit farms throughout the area. I was so taken with the place that I had thought of getting into the fruit-growing business in the long term. The outdoor life, and working in such a beautiful place appealed to me. It never happened though. Life took me elsewhere. After a little searching, I found a job picking seasonal fruit. At that time I believe it may have been plums but I picked other fruit from time to time depending on the season.

The accommodation was not a problem as I was given the use of a large cabin to sleep in. I was not alone however as I found that the room was also occupied by a group of about eight French Canadians from Quebec who were also there following the same menial occupation as me. When the day was over, we would all retire to the cabin and they would jabber away far too quickly for me to pick up anything from my few years of school French. I couldn't make out what on earth they were talking about. Once in a while, though one of them would turn to me and say,

"Hey, English! What you think? How long you gonna stay?" or some such question. I was always 'Hey English' to them whenever I was included. I stayed there for a few days and discovered quickly that you can barely make enough money picking fruit to even feed yourself, but I stuck at it for a while and soon the French Voyageurs were gone, presumably by canoe, but no sooner had they departed, than they were replaced by another traveller in the form of a large Irishman named Brian who was wandering through North America.

We became pals briefly and picked fruit together, swapping tales. We were both disappointed in the rewards of fruit picking and at the end of one day as we walked back along the road a pickup truck pulled up alongside us and asked if we wanted a job at the sawmill. The prospects were certainly better than what we had been doing, and with a wage that we had no hope of equalling picking fruit. We took the chance, said, "Yes.", and were all go. We would start that very night on the night shift, so we grabbed a quick snack at the little town cafe and signed on at the sawmill.

When we arrived there I didn't know where Brian had gone. He disappeared, but I was sent to the 'green chain'. The green chain is where they often put starters and is the meanest, toughest roughest body-breaking job there is in the mill. It was the toughest work that I have ever done in my life. The sawmill was producing planks of wood, of various widths and thicknesses, all fed onto a conveyor belt, and my job, as the green-chain man, was to pick them up and stack them onto various piles according to size. They were heavy. Oh boy!, they were so heavy, and within half an hour I was completely worn out as I staggered from pile to pile.

The planks were all falling off the end of the chain onto the floor in a pile that was getting bigger all the time. There was no way that I could keep up. I just wanted it to end. I wanted to transport myself to some sunny beach in Tahiti with those beautiful girls, but no, there I was staggering under the weight of a huge plank that I could barely lift, finding the right pile to put it on, struggling to get in on top and watching it topple off while the conveyor belt delivered more and more to be deposited on the floor with the others. I was half dead. I remembered my dad's words. He was a religious man, often quoting from the bible and he would say to me,

"Jim, you don't want to be a 'hewer of wood, or a drawer of water.'"

Yes, Dad, you were right. I had been picking fruit all day,

which didn't help, but I don't think that it would have made much difference. We were on the eight o'clock to four a.m. shift and mercifully a bell went off at around midnight. It was time for a meal break. I went to the canteen where I met up again with Brian. I don't know where he had been, and as I sat there wearily I said to him,

"How you doin'?"

"Tired," he said.

"I think I'm gonna quit," I said.

"Thank God for that," he replied, "but I wasn't gonna quit before you." He was a big guy and didn`t want to be the first to drop. " Come on, let's go." So we did.

So I worked half a shift on the green chain, and if you tell anybody that, who's in the know, they might well buy you a drink on the strength of it. That was it. It was time to head back to Vancouver.

I then got a job in the boomerang factory. That probably sounds odd, but it's true. It was just another episode in my long and varied career. A very enterprising South African man had come to Vancouver and was convinced that he was going to make a killing at the P.N.E., (The Pacific National Exhibition), a big annual event in Vancouver with traders' stalls and amusements. He was going to manufacture thousands of boomerangs which he would sell there and make his fortune, and who better to employ to make them than a bunch of hippies? So I joined with a small group of my hippy friends to work in a small factory in North Vancouver, where we all took on different tasks in their manufacture. We cut the boomerangs from large sheets of plywood. One guy would cut the raw shapes with a band saw, I would shape the edges with a router, the next guy would sand them smooth, and then the girl hippies would stain them, stick on decals, and varnish them. This was all done as a large-scale production and we made many thousands of boomerangs.

It was very interesting to see what made a boomerang work and to learn just why they flew and why they returned (sometimes). In principle, the boomerang consists of two aerofoils, like aeroplane wings, which is what gives them lift, but because of their shape and spin there is also a centrifugal force which makes them twist in flight, and so, if you are lucky, return to you.

We experimented with the blade shapes to optimize their performance until we perfected them. My friends and I would take a bunch of them to the park and have great fun throwing them, but it was a dangerous game as the light was fading when boomerangs were whistling past your ears or thumping into your legs. I enjoyed that little episode in my life. It was great fun being children again and playing with our toys. But when the P.N.E. came along so did the Frisbee, so that was that.

The jobs that I had throughout those times were all ones that required no brain. It would be some time before I found anything that I could apply myself to. They just paid the bills and that was enough for me at the time.

* * *

PART 3

* * *

22

SUE

Then I met Sue and my life was about to take another major change of direction.

I met Sue on a blind date through Cousin Brendan's girlfriend who was keen to set us up together., so we met up and went to a party one evening. It was summertime, warm and beautiful, and all went swimmingly. We were attracted to each other, one thing led to another and we started going out together. Sue was blonde and very attractive to me and we hit it off right away. We saw a lot of each other in the days that followed and soon after that first blind date, we moved in together. She was a quiet home-loving girl and her greatest loves in life were her family and her home space. So we set about homemaking. We were happy together in our small apartment, acquiring bits of furniture to add to the place, mostly from charity shops as money was always in short supply.

It was a new experience for both of us. I remember making a rather wobbly coffee table, from which one of the legs kept falling off. It was not very successful but it gave us and our visitors many laughs. My carpentry skills were not the best on that one, but my next project with wood, which I will come to shortly, was far more successful.

Sue introduced me to her family, a younger brother and two younger sisters who were living in White Rock, a few miles south of Vancouver. Her parents were divorced but were still good friends, and her dad, Reg Romero was a well-known local actor. He performed with 'The White Rock Players' theatrical group and was appearing in adverts on TV.

Until that time in my life, I had not been a theatre-goer but Sue and I would go along to see the shows that her dad was in and on to the parties that always followed. It was a good life and I could see that Reg was a very fine actor. We saw him once in a leading role in "My Fair Lady" which impressed me very much. He had had some minor roles in film in England before emigrating to Canada. He later had an ongoing role in the Canadian TV production called "The Beachcombers" He was a fun guy and always kept us amused in one way or another, like with his staged trips on entering the room. He was by nature a performer and comedian.

Sue on our trip through Oregon en route to California

Sue

Oregon coast in the mist

Travels with an old guitar

Then Sue got pregnant. This was a life-changing event for us both. We had been quite content as we were, drifting along in our hippy world, just enjoying our lives, but with a baby on the way, we had to make some decisions. Responsibility loomed on the horizon. What should we do?

We decided to get married. It seemed the right thing to do. We still maintained our connections with our many friends from that hippy world but life for us now had taken on a different flavour. I was no longer a single, carefree man who could wander where he pleased at his own pace. No longer a tumbling tumbleweed. It was time to take on more responsibility. This was quite a transition for me as I had always been quite a solitary person, going where the spirit moved me, so I had to readjust to a different lifestyle altogether. It was a big transition for Sue too as she had still been living with her family in White Rock until we moved in together. We had unexpectedly been propelled into a new world of responsibility. I was about to become 'Dad' and enter yet another new phase in this exciting life'

I wrote to my family back in England telling them of my news, and this was the final event that led my mum to decide to come out to Canada too to join her two faraway sons. Her second marriage had not worked out for her so she was free to travel, which she had always wanted to do. Now she had the excuse to do just that. I had seen that part in her that longed to travel long ago when I first left her and England. four years earlier. So with this news in mind, Sue and I delayed our wedding for a month until Mum arrived. Meanwhile, Sue expanded.

Sue

Mum would never entertain the idea of flying so we had to wait for her journey across the Atlantic on an ocean liner, followed by a train journey right across the country. Meanwhile Sue continued to expand. We were fortunate enough to get the very next apartment to ours for her, so she would be close by as she was planning to stay.

So a new episode in my life started. Mum arrived safely, Sue and I got married in the registry office in Vancouver with all of our family present, followed by a trip to Reg's house in White Rock for a party where we all got to know each other properly.

So it's married life for Jim.

23

JOE

1969 was a big year. It was the year that men first landed on the moon which was an amazing thing to see. My brother Paul and I, Sue, and Mum watched it live on TV in Mum's apartment and were quite enthralled to watch this historic event as it unfolded.

But more amazing still to me was that my son Joe was born that year. This was something that turned my life around. I had made adjustments to being a married man, but being a father was something else. Suddenly my priorities changed drastically, and my values changed from the moment that he was born. Here was this tiny baby, my son, who would need my care and attention. It was the furthest thing from hardship to me and I discovered that he was now the thing that mattered most to me in my life. Hanging around with my buddies and playing music together was still fun but it was not so important anymore. All I wanted was to be a Dad and to do my best for baby Joe. Having a son had added a whole new dimension to my life. It changed me overnight, and I took to it like a duck to water. I just loved it.

The family were enthralled with him too and came to visit at the first opportunity. Joe was a good-natured happy baby, who cried sometimes as babies do, but he was not a distressed child, and as he grew he was forever laughing. It was wonderful.

After working at all those meaningless jobs I was now seeking a bit more direction, especially now that I had a family to look after. I had a brain but had never really used it. My work had been unskilled requiring just my two hands and very little else.

My educational qualifications were minimal with just one GCE from my schooling in England as I had taken the minimum number of subjects necessary and hadn't even tried much in my exams. I had been lazy in my final year at school. There had been nobody to push me, guide me, and help me make a sensible decision or tell me about the value of education.

The career that I was now looking at was Surveying. It appealed to me for several reasons. I was good at maths, which would be a necessary part of the work and the job entailed outdoor activity, so it seemed to me to be the best of both worlds. It was much more appealing than working in an office which I had already found to be quite stifling and unsatisfying. I was inspired by the idea and found that there was a course at the local Technical Institute where I could get the required training.

The entry requirements required more qualifications than those I had, so I made inquiries from the education board of B.C. as to how much I was deficient. As a result of their assessment, I took on two courses by correspondence, one in English Literature, and one in New Maths. The English Literature course was fascinating and I loved it. It filled a gap in my knowledge of the writings in our language, going back to the earliest forms. I did not take to the New Maths though. It seemed to go around the houses to describe things and I never did see the light at the end of the tunnel.

I progressed well, but unfortunately, my plans for a surveying career did not pan out the way that I had hoped. The hard reality was that I could not support a family and go to school without Sue going out to work. This had been in the plan but in the end, she felt unable to do that. She had taken to the advice she was given by her mother that married women should not have to work. That was that. So I had to shelve the idea, and a Surveyor I was not to be. It was a great disappointment to me, and it would be some years yet until I could get into a more worthwhile occupation, and not be in my dad's words a "Hewer of Wood". But such is life.

It was time that I started driving again, so I took my driving test for British Columbia and bought myself a 1958 Volkswagen Beetle. I adored that car and it was great to have mobility again. It was sky blue and in need of a paint job, so Sue and I bought a dozen spray cans and painted it one windless day, after which Sue painted a big white flower on the back. We were living in flower power days! It looked like, and was, a car for those times.

We chugged around in that little beetle enjoying our new mobility but had one memorable experience in it. We went to see a drive-in movie, sat in the back, and settled down to watch the film but after a while, I noticed a smell of burning, and smoke began to appear from beneath us. We jumped out of the car and I hauled the back seat out which was then smouldering. I managed to put it out in a puddle and then I could see what had caused the problem. The battery in those old beetles sits under the back seat, and I had forgotten to put the cover back on top. When we had sat in the back, the springs on the underside of the seat had shorted the battery out, causing the fire. It was a great little car though and served us well. The back wheel teetered on the end of the axle and almost fell off on us once as I hurtled along the motorway but I still loved it and kept it for several years.

The next job that I got was working for the BC Liquor Control Board in the warehouse where all of the liquor is collected together in one place, from local manufacturers and overseas suppliers, and from there, it is distributed throughout the province.

Liquor in B.C., like the rest of Canada, was only sold under strict conditions and the Provincial government had it under wraps. My job was just menial labour but not too heavy and each day brought me a different task. I was able to do the job well enough even though many of my work colleagues were built like oxen compared to me.

Although these jobs that I was drifting through were little more than manual labour, it was always interesting to talk with my fellows. At the liquor board, I would often spend the whole day with the same three or four guys, some of them on a break from university so the social part was very worthwhile. I always enjoyed the mental stimulation even though the work was mundane. Wherever you go, whatever you do, it's always people that make life so interesting.

Drinking at work was forbidden and if you were caught drinking or drunk you would be fired instantly. However, rules are made to be broken and on many occasions, I would get the word that a bottle was on the go in a far corner of the warehouse, so I got to sample some very fine liquor and developed a taste for good Port. The money was good there, better than I had been able to earn anywhere since arriving in Canada.

After Joe had been born and was still a baby, Sue and I moved out to the White Rock area where her parents lived. I liked the area as it was away from the bustle of Vancouver and we leased a house in Crescent Beach.

The sensible thing would have been to buy a house there as it was quite affordable then and would have been a good move. The prices since those days have gone up into the millions but we could have bought something nice for just a few thousand dollars. Crescent Beach was a lovely spot where Sue had grown up, with sandy beaches and it suited us well. We had a small single-story house and garden which was ideal for us. Unfortunately, we only had the house for a time-limited period as the owners occupied it for a couple of months in the summer.

When the lease was up we found another little house nearby, as there were always plenty of rentals available. It was a good spot to be living in and good for Sue, as her whole family was in that area. I had taken to rural living, away from city life. Joe was a growing little boy by then and was a delight to all, and especially to me. He was such a happy little chap.

I found it so easy to relate to him, and I took huge delight in sharing with him his discovery of the world. I found that I could revert to being a child again myself and I loved it. We didn't have a great deal of money but we were managing and were a happy little family.

It was while we were living in that house that I got the idea of building a kayak. I had a book that contained all the detailed plans for the project, which consisted of making the internal structure from thin strips of wood and then covering it with canvas. I set to work constructing it in the back garden, where it gradually took shape under a canopy that I had constructed. I had never made anything like that before but I had learned some woodworking skills at school and they served me well.

So eventually, after months of work, I had the skeleton of a kayak. I bought some canvas to finish it off, painted it, added

Joe

two seats and a footrest and it was done. I was very proud of the finished product and when I took it down to the river and cautiously put it in, climbed in, and paddled off I was amazed at how light, stable, and manoeuvrable it was. It had taken me long months to finish and at the time of the grand launching, Joe had told me that as he stood on the riverbank he was suddenly very worried about his dad taking off into the river. We christened the boat, 'Jenny', but the real Jenny was yet to come.

My musical interests never left me and it was then that I first took an interest in the five-string banjo, and ever since those far-off days, I have always had a banjo close at hand, and nowadays I play the banjo as much as the guitar. It is a fascinating instrument and quite addictive.

Life was sailing along quite nicely for our little family. I bought a Volkswagen Camper van, as we had the idea of getting away at weekends, which we did locally in B.C., but we had larger ambitions. I had a holiday from my job at the Liquor Board so we planned another trip to California.

We made preparations, packed up the van with all that we might need, and set off on the highway heading South to the sun. Unfortunately though, as we approached Seattle on a long hill, the engine blew up. I had my kayak on the top of the van, which I was not going to abandon after all that work, so we had to phone for assistance and got a tow to Seattle, where our best option was to have a reconditioned engine installed. That used up all of my money, so we turned around and headed home. California would have to wait.

So all was well with us. I had a fairly good well-paid job, we had a home, and a car and all of our immediate needs were met. But then, soon after our aborted trip to California, we made a decision that we would go to England for a visit. I wanted to show off Joe to my family. He was my Dad's first grandson, and Sue was keen to go and see the country where she had been born. She had emigrated to Canada as a young girl with her parents and liked the idea of going for a visit.

I managed to get a leave of absence from the Liquor Board so that I would have a job to come back to, so not all of our boats would be burned. The choice that we had then was to either put our money down on a house, or take a trip to England, but you know by now how sensible or otherwise my choices often turn out to be. So we made our plans.

* * *

24

FRANCE - JENNY

There were plenty of cheap air flights available in 1971. We had not yet entered the era of huge jumbo jets, so we travelled on a Boeing 707. Those planes could not do the whole distance to England from Vancouver in one leap, so had to stop in Iceland or Greenland to refuel for the final part of the journey. On this trip, we stopped at Reykjavik in Iceland. Neither Sue, nor I, nor Joe who was then two years old had flown before so it was a new experience for all of us. We were all a bit apprehensive, but once we started trundling down the runway and began to lift off I was enthralled. I thought it was great and turned excitedly to Sue and said,

"Wow! Look at that." While I watched everything shrink in size below us. Sue was petrified and kept her eyes firmly in front of her, clutching the seat, and refused to look. Joe was okay and very wide-eyed. In those days you could elect to sit in 'smoking' or 'non-smoking' areas, and the alcohol flowed freely. People would wander about smoking, drinking and partying. It was great fun, but I learned quickly that, for me at least, it was better not to drink booze on flights.

Iceland was the bleakest-looking place that I had ever seen. The landscape as we approached and left the airport was brown. Everything was brown. It looked desolate and not at all appealing We had to leave the plane and walk across the tarmac to a building that housed us while they re-fuelled the plane, and when that was done we took off again to complete the last part of our flight successfully, much to Sue's relief, and descended on our approach to Gatwick Airport.

I looked out of the window and saw the green fields of the English countryside again which I confess brought a tear to my eye. I still felt a great kinship with this land of mine where I had been born and grew up. It had been five years since I had left and the memories came flooding back.

Customs were simple and soon we were surrounded by people who spoke just like me. It sounded odd since I had been surrounded by Canadians for the past five years. I caught the sound of accents that were entrenched in the South of England with inflexions that I recognised. It was a strange feeling, a mix of kinship, and at the same time of being a foreign visitor.

We caught a slow train to Brighton. It was sunny and warm, and the train made its way South, stopping almost everywhere. I remember catching the idle chatter of two old ladies who were sitting near us cutting through the silence. Their accents and manner of speech amused me. It was England that I knew so well and gave me a warm feeling of familiarity. For Sue and Joe, it must have been very different from the world that they knew back in Canada.

We arrived in Brighton, collected our luggage, and as we came off the platform out into the station, it was wonderful to see Mum, who had come back to England, and my lovely

Aunts, Rusty and Vida who had played a big part in my childhood. The wanderer had returned, complete with a family.

Joe was a huge hit with his Canadian accent, and they welcomed Sue warmly as a part of our family. We got a taxi to Mum's flat in Compton Avenue, the very road where I was born. It was a homecoming for me and I was quite overwhelmed by the feeling of kinship. Mum had a spare room which would be our base. We spent the next few hours re-acquainting and meeting other members of the family, but the jet lag eventually caught up with us big time, until we were asleep standing and could not hold out any longer. We crashed out to sleep, well into the next day.

We wanted to make the most of our trip, so I bought a large Bedford van within a few days of arriving, which we rigged with a mattress, a heater, and a few supplies ready for our voyage of exploration. Sue wanted to visit Wales, where her mum had come from, and where she had only recently discovered that she had some half-siblings from her Dad's former marriage. She had known nothing about them until her dad told her just before we had come on this trip. So about a week later, we set off from Brighton travelling West.

We had our accommodation on wheels so travel was easy and we stopped here and there to enjoy whatever we found in an unhurried way. We stopped in Somerset and indulged ourselves in the local cider and scrumpy. It was lovely and so English. I felt like a tourist. We visited Cheddar Gorge and other places of interest, then crossed the River Severn into Wales and explored the Wye Valley.

The countryside was so beautiful. British Columbia

scenery is majestic and beautiful but this scenery had a different kind of gentle beauty. Unfortunately, we had no success in our efforts to locate Sue's siblings in South Wales so we moved on, crossing Wales from East to West, intending to go across the water to Ireland for a few days, but the ferry fare for our van was outrageous and not worth our while, so we opted for just staying in beautiful Wales for a while longer. Wales was new to me too as I had never been there before. It appeared to be full of sheep.

It was very pleasant being tourists and we spent a week or two on the road visiting towns and scenic spots in Wales and the South West of England enjoying ourselves in everything English and then it was back to Brighton for some more family time.

Sue and I wanted to see something of the continent of Europe while we were visiting, so after another stay in Brighton, we packed up the van and made our way to Dover for the ferry crossing to France.

The sea was rough on that short journey though and we were all under the weather from the tossing around of the ferry. Poor Joe was seasick and didn't know what was happening to him, but it was all over within a few hours and we were soon on French soil. We planned to travel down through France and into Spain, but our estimate of the distance was way out, so having travelled South as far as the town of Lille we decided that in the limited time we had, it was not very sensible to drive to Spain, so we opted for more of France.

We were cooking for ourselves with a small gas cooker that we carried on board, and one day Sue and I had a yen for some sausages, so went into a butcher's shop to buy some. I had had a few years of French at school, but I was a long way from being fluent, so I had the devil of a time trying to describe to the butcher what I wanted. I had no idea what 'Sausage' was in French, so I started miming, showing the shape of a sausage and using the word, 'Cochon' which I did remember was 'pig'. "No, I don't want a pig, just a bit of pig in a tube." Eventually, after lots of gesticulating, the butcher said ' "Ah!" and beckoned me to follow him. He spoke to me but that was not much use. Meanwhile, Mrs. Butcher, Sue, and Joe just smiled at each other. I followed him to a side room where he proceeded to make me some sausages, or rather, he made me a sausage. He got some sort of skin for it, filled it, and made me one very long object about three feet long. We said our 'Merci's' and left. When we stopped later to cook it, we had great amusement trying to cut it, and eat it as we found that the skin was almost impenetrable; it was a devil of a job to cut, and even harder on the teeth. We decided not to bother with sausages again until we got back to England.

We moved on further North towards Belgium and as night came on we found a place to park almost outside a house on the edge of town. We slept well, and when we woke up the following morning as I was stretching outside the van, an elderly lady from the house came out. I thought at first that she was going to tell me off for parking there outside her house, but it wasn't that at all. My French was not a great deal of use to me most of the time, but I gradually picked up enough of what she was saying to realize that she was inviting me, Sue and Joe, in to have a shower. I couldn't believe the kindness.

Maybe it was when she had seen Joe that she made the offer. I was so cautious of misinterpreting what she had said to me, but sure enough, that is what she was saying. So we all trooped into her house and she showed us to the bathroom. The bidet was a confusing item and caused more amusement for us, but it was lovely to have a shower. We were able to have a good clean-up, and this was followed by coffee with our hostess.

The lady took great interest when we told her that we were from Canada. As I looked around her living room I noticed a photo of a young man. I said to her,

"C'est votre fils?" My best attempt to ask if it was her son.

"Oui," she replied. "Il est mort." I thought I knew what she was saying but it would be dreadful to make a mistake here. I had to be very careful.

"Il est Morte?"

"Oui." With some difficulty, she managed to convey to me that he had been killed in a motorcycle accident. How tragic. She was such a lovely lady. Sue spoke not a word of French so I translated for her and after spending a little more time with her we made our Au Revoirs and off we went.

Throughout my travels, there were so many times when I encountered such kindness. Most people are good at heart and you don't even have to speak the same language.

Although my French was poor at best I thought I was doing OK. I was managing to get the supplies that we needed, like bread, milk, sausages of a sort, etc. Arm gestures didn't help much. They just raised frowns.

I needed some oil for the van and hadn't come across a

garage, so I thought that I would ask somewhere. We came across a pub and went in. There were about six guys in there and they all looked up when I walked in. I tried to ask them where I might get some oil, whereupon they all burst out laughing, almost rolling on the floor. I don't know what I said, but obviously, it was hilarious to them and I had failed. I left with my head hung in shame.

But Joe was doing OK. I had been freely handing out "Merci's" all over the place, and he was soon following me doing the same, often followed by some "Au Revoir's" thrown in too, which the French people took great delight in.

We drove straight into Belgium without finding any border checks at all and spent a day there but Belgium was not so different from France in our eyes. There was not much that interested us there so we turned around and went back into France. From there made our way through the country and across the sea once more to the White Cliffs of Dover, where they spoke a language that I could manage and they knew what sausages were.

Auntie Vida had been knitting big time, making small things for Joe and before we went home to Canada we had accumulated a great many jumpers in a variety of colours and styles. So many in fact that we had trouble packing everything into the cases that we had. The aunts had no children and they thrived on having Joe to fuss over. They had done the same for me as a boy growing up and it was a real pleasure for them to continue this with Joe.

We had a fabulous time, squeezing a lot into our six-week stay in England and Europe, but the time came for us to go back home to Canada. We started the return journey from Brighton Station, accompanied by Mum and the Aunts who were there to see us off. We had one unfortunate mishap there for as we were saying goodbye from the train, we slammed the big steel door shut right onto Sue's hand. The poor girl was in agony.

So we left Brighton bound for the airport. It was supposed to be Gatwick Airport but our flight details had been altered and instead of leaving from Gatwick to Vancouver, we were re-routed to fly from Stanstead Airport to Seattle, and on top of that our flight did not leave until around 5 am, so it became a marathon journey.

Eventually, we departed from Stanstead but had a further problem when we got to Seattle. I had a British passport, but no Visa for the USA. I told the authorities that I lived in Canada and had crossed the border many times from there but they were sticklers for obeying rules. Flying into the USA from Europe on a British passport meant that I had to have a visa and that was that. No exceptions. So I was escorted through the airport by a policeman with a gun on his hip to the coach that had been laid on for us. I felt like a criminal and I imagine that the people in the airport must have thought the same. Jim the felon being taken away. I should have shouted something and made a show of it, but I didn't. It was not a good idea to antagonise the authorities with an armed cop by my side. The cop handed my passport to the bus driver and said,

"Don't let him get off the bus until he gets to Canada."

So after a journey of nearly 24 hours, we finally got back

to our little home. We were wiped out, but it was very good to be home. We had had a marvellous, very satisfying trip to England and Europe and to meet up with my family again and show off Joe and Sue

We settled back into our Canadian lives once more after that marvellous trip. I still had my job at the Liquor Board, and life rolled on very pleasantly for us in White Rock.

Then a month or two later we found that Sue was pregnant again, and in February of 1972, our daughter Jenny entered the world.

Our family was growing, and we both loved being parents. We now had a boy and a girl. Joe and Jenny were both blondes like their mum and when they were small their hair got even fairer with the sun. Sue was never a talkative person but both Joe and Jenny made up for it in a big way as they grew and always had plenty to say. They were entertaining, intelligent, and always great company. I have been so proud of them both.

Joe had naturally gravitated to me, and Jenny to her mum in those early days. Maybe it's about gender, I don't know, but anyway, that's what happened. I had a fantastic rapport with Joe, and we did lots of things together right from the start. I loved every moment of being Dad and sharing in his discovery of the world around us together. But Jenny was different. I believe that somehow in her young brain, she had got the notion that I was the creature from the Black Lagoon. She screamed every time I came near her.

Baby Jenny

Maybe she just favoured the protection of Mum, but certainly, in those early days, I had great difficulty in getting through to her. I don't know why. But I am so pleased to say that that was only an early phase and as the years went by Jenny and I formed a great relationship. She was always a girl who wanted to do things for herself. She has always had confidence in her own ability. She was small and dainty and very girlish. I didn't understand those girly ways, but I was very happy just being her Dad.

We had had a wonderful time in England and together Sue and I made the decision that we would like to go to live there for a while, just for a year or two, and so we made our plans to return the following year. This would also turn into a major turning point in my life but I had no crystal ball to show me what lay ahead.

It was at that point that I made one of life's serious blunders. I was a safely landed immigrant with residency status, but I had not taken out the precaution of becoming a citizen, which I could so easily have done and the result was that for most of my life thereafter I had difficulty re-entering Canada and staying for any length of time. While I was in England the rules on residency had changed.

* * *

25

ENGLAND

So that brings me to the end of my first adventurous eight years in Canada. If I had stayed where I was in Brighton and worked in the legal profession my life would have no doubt been very different. Who knows where it would have taken me? But I don't regret for one moment my decision to step onboard that ship way back there in 1964 and to have been through those times that ensued. I had a great life wandering about discovering myself and the world.

But the story doesn't end there. Life moved on and so did I. I wasn't done yet with travelling, so the following is a summary of how life's deck of cards played out further for me over the following years.

I am writing this from my house in Lymington, Hampshire, where I have been for more years than I anticipated. I never expected to be here, or even to be in England again, but I have found that life sometimes takes you where you don't expect it to. Life has nevertheless been good to me here. I still have my guitars and banjos and I still play music with friends. I have played in bands in the pubs and have even been a local busker with a couple of pals. Singing and playing have been a lifelong love for me. That old Indian, Geronimo could rightly have called me "Travels With An Old Guitar"

Fred   Jim   Bob   - Busking in more recent times.

So to continue my story. Sue, Joe, Jenny and I came back to England in 1974. We went to my hometown of Brighton again and rented a flat in the same house as Mum and my aunts on the same road where I was born. It had been a very long round trip for me.

I got a job as a postman which entailed very early morning starts, which was pretty awful. But on a fine summer's early morning, it was marvellous to be out and about near the Brighton countryside. It was tough work though, hauling two heavy bags of mail to their destinations.

We had a good life being close to my relatives, spending time with my dad again, and my brother Ronn and his wife, Daphne and so we settled back to life in England. Joe and

Travels with an old guitar

Jenny went to school and found new friends.

After all those years of doing manual jobs I at last found a career that suited me. I had applied myself to the study of electronics, taken a course in that field and had become qualified in that trade. I was working in the field of television, video recorder and audio equipment servicing. I had, at last, found a field where I could use my brain instead of my muscles. I am sure that Dad was delighted that I was no longer in his words a "Hewer of Wood".

We had a few good years in Brighton. Christmas came and. Sue's mum, dad and brother came over to stay with us, and a great time was had by all, but soon after that visit another big change came.

Sue had decided to return to Canada. I was not a part of that decision. She had decided she wanted to go with the children to be near her family again. I suppose she had had some discussions with her family about all this on their visit. So it was a parting of ways for us.

I had not seen it coming as she didn't tell me what she was feeling. It was just presented as a "fait accomplis". She was homesick for Canada and her close family. I intended to follow so that I could at least be near my kids. They meant the world to me, but I had a problem as I had lost my Canadian residency status, having been away from Canada for too long. I tried to get back there, but it proved to be very difficult without Sue's cooperation which was not forthcoming so all I could do was to carry on with my life in England for the time being.

England

I would visit the pubs frequently and watch the Brighton bands, some of whom I remembered from when I was playing there myself. Meanwhile, I must have explored every curry house in town. I still had my job but my goal was always to return to Canada. I had no intention of becoming detached from my children indefinitely.

I spent a whole year trying to overcome this problem and after unsuccessful attempts to regain my status there by visiting the Canadian embassy in London where I was simply told that I had made my choice, I simply quit my job and bought a ticket as a visitor. I could not wait any longer.

Sue had moved up North in BC to a town called Smithers, along with her whole family. I will need to go into some detail about what follows as it had a profound effect on all of us.

When I got back to Canada I phoned my mother-in-law, Anne who warned me that I should get myself up there quickly. She told me that she was concerned for the children's welfare so I took a flight, booked into a motel, and went to visit her. She told me that she thought it would be in the children's best interest for me to take the children to live with me. This was something that I didn't anticipate, especially coming from my mother-in-law. Sue was having problems of her own and was having difficulty looking after them. Joe had been having to help Jenny get dressed in the morning.

My mother-in-law, Anne, called for Joe and Jenny to come over saying she had a surprise for them.

When they walked in it was a wonderful moment for me after being away from them for a year. My kids were my world. Jenny barely remembered me but Joe did, of course, and Jenny just followed his lead.

I went to see Sue, and that was a difficult meeting. We had a short discussion in a darkened room and she agreed that it would be in their best interests if I should take them with me. She offered no resistance. Her sister June was pleading with her not to let this happen. It must have been hard for Sue, but she only wanted the best for them, and she knew that I would be dedicated to their welfare and could give them a better life than she could, and that's all I can say about that. I told her that I might have to take them back to England as I was not even a legal resident of Canada anymore, and she did not object.

So Joe, Jenny, and I took the long journey back to Vancouver on the Greyhound to start a new life together. I had not anticipated this but I was a very happy man. I loved my children and it had fallen into my lap to take them on with me. It would be hard but I was quite ready for the task.

Joe was seven and Jenny was four.

We stayed with my brother Paul for a couple of weeks while I tried to decide my best course of action. Either to stay in Canada and fight through the courts for the right to remain in Canada, which would be a hard drawn out process, or to return to England where I would have my family's support. I made the decision to return to England with the children.

So that's how I became a single parent. I am pleased to say that our lives have forever been close, even though after they had grown up we were frequently many miles apart. My greatest pleasure in life right from the start was being their Dad, and in the early days of being a single parent, I took on the responsibility of being their caring guardian as my number one priority. It was complete fulfilment for me to be the one that they needed and I did the very best that I could for them, although of course, I made occasional mistakes, as we all do. I had to fulfil the role of both parents somehow.

Although Jenny was so young when that parting happened, the loss of her mother had a deep effect on her, which she carried with her for years, and I have to take some responsibility for that. even though we went on to have a happy life together, and she was a happy little girl. I did what seemed right at the time, but there was a price to pay. Joe seemed to be able to ride through anything, but he was always a very sensitive boy with deep feelings and may well have carried his thoughts about that time deep inside him. When we speak of it now they tell me that there is no doubt that I did the right thing.

My lovely children Jenny and Joe in Brighton

Travels with an old guitar

Their lives with Sue would have been very different and their prospects were going downhill in a bad way.

We came to live in England again where I was fortunate enough to go back to my old job and have the help of my mum and my aunts, whose lives were greatly enriched by having Joe and Jenny around them. Consequently, they became very close to their Granny for the rest of her life.

As time went on. Joe and Jenny were making friends and we got them into the same school in Brighton that I had been to as a boy. Joe happily adjusted to being an English boy and was great company for me too. We used to go fishing together, sometimes with my dad which was a pleasure for us all. Joe was my dad's first and only grandson. Jenny was a little girl with a very creative mind of her own, and she no longer thought I was the creature from the black lagoon.

The aunts adored her. They had loved having Joe with them when we had first visited and they still did, but now they also had a little girl. They were in heaven. They doted on her, and she thrived on it. My auntie Kit, another of Mum's sisters, made Jenny a rag doll which she has to this day. She called it "Base", and when we asked her, "Why Base?" she replied, "For the Bay City Rollers" It made sense to Jenny. So "Base" it has remained and it still looks out in Jenny's room from a much-faded face, that got all but erased once in the washing machine.

England

* * *

26

JUNE - NEW ZEALAND

Then another romance entered my life. I met June. And so began another new episode of this grand adventure.

I had been on my own for a while so it was refreshing to have a new interesting partner, and to share things with June. She was a great thinker. She was intelligent, and I was able to have interesting discussions with her on all sorts of things which is something that I had missed. So we linked up and moved in together to a house in Lancing, Sussex.

June had two boys, Carl and Austin from her first marriage, whose ages slotted in with Joe and Jenny's. The age sequence was Joe, Carl, Jenny, and Austin.

Being a step-parent can bring difficulties, as anyone knows who has undergone this change, and we had a few of those but we did pretty well in general. I was devoted to my two children and now had to learn to also be a step-parent, as did June, but we did amalgamate quite well and soon built a life together.

June was a trained Nursery Nurse and apart from working in childcare nurseries, she looked after young children occasionally in our home which was wonderful for all of us.

We became very attached to those lovely wee ones. They became almost family to us.

June was an only child and had a strict upbringing with very little freedom. She had never travelled across the world as I had and was somewhat envious of my experiences of freedom.

We had a lot in common though and soon found that we had a similar dream. Throughout my life, I have been inclined to wander but now I found a new goal. I wanted to see New Zealand, a place that had intrigued me for years. It had all the magnificent beauty of British Columbia in a warmer climate. But there was a lot more to it than that. I had read a great deal about the country and the culture there appealed to me. It was not overpopulated and people had an easygoing attitude to life. It appeared to me to be just the place for a good life.

June was completely with me on this enterprise. It was to be a joint venture as we planned to abandon our life in England to head South in search of better times for us and the children.

We were living in a council house on a fairly new estate, which had not yet run down the way they often do, but there is no doubt that our prospects were limited. We could not then afford to buy a house of any reasonable size and the council house environment we felt was not the best for our four children to grow up in. New Zealand represented a much better future for us all.

We had several obstacles to overcome first though to achieve our dream. Firstly, June's parents were not at all keen on us leaving. They said to her,

Travels with an old guitar

"Well that's it, we will never see you again."

It was a tough one for her. The second obstacle we faced was that to take Carl and Austin to the other side of the world we would need the permission of Andy, their dad. However, we were on the best of terms with him. He and I always got on very well together and he did not object. He also saw it as a good opportunity for them.

We also needed the permission of Joe and Jenny's mum, Sue in Canada, but this too presented no problem either and she agreed

There was one further roadblock for us and that was that the New Zealand government would only accept us if we were a married couple. So we married.

I had to work and study hard to follow that dream by taking more exams to acquire the qualifications that I needed in my field of electronics. I did well and achieved distinction level in them all. I enjoyed applying myself to serious studies.

I then wrote to many TV companies in New Zealand and one of the national companies offered me a job and offered to pay for our airfares. There were not enough qualified electronics technicians in the field of TV and VCRs in the country to fulfil their needs.

So we were home free and ready for the grand adventure. We knew nobody in New Zealand so it was a bold step for us all.

We made our plans and carefully packed all of our worldly possessions for shipping. Then it was a grand departure at Gatwick Airport with a multitude of family members and friends to see us off, accompanied by many tears as we set off on our journey into the unknown with four young children in tow. I had been freewheeling for a long time but now I also had a large family to consider. It gave me plenty of thought to consider the rights or wrongs of such a move.

We stopped in Los Angeles on the way there and took the kids to Disneyland which gave us all a huge thrill. June and the kids had never been, and for me, I was once more in the "Magic Kingdom". It was as uplifting of the spirits as it ever was. Thank you so much, Uncle Walt!

After that delightful interlude and the endless flight across the Pacific, stopping briefly in Hawaii, we arrived in Auckland to start our new life.

My first impressions of Auckland were good. The people were indeed easygoing and friendly. The presence of the Maori culture is all around you which is a delight. The accent also hits you right away. The New Zealanders have switched around vowel pronunciation considerably but one soon adapted to that. after initial confusion.

I worked temporarily in the firm's base in Auckland getting used to repairing the TVs that were common there, while June and the children got to explore the local territory. The firm had put us up in a motel and all expenses were paid, so we spent the next two weeks acclimatising.

The firm offered us a choice of towns where I could go to work. Auckland's house prices were beyond us as were several other cities in the North Island, so we chose Dunedin on the South Island, where we could more easily afford to buy a house large enough for our big family.

Travels with an old guitar

I did find myself wondering at first if I had done the right thing. It was winter, it was cold and we had to deal with a certain amount of culture shock. We had taken the kids away from their schools, friends, grandparents, aunts and familiar land into the unknown. It was a big responsibility for June and me, but these worries were only temporary. and after a short while, we adjusted and things improved for us greatly.

My firm looked after us well, gave me a car and set us up with temporary accommodation.

The first few weeks in Mosgiel, a small town just South of Dunedin where we had decided to live were a challenge for us. We rented a house that was very basic, very uniform in layout like so many houses there with a central hallway and all rooms leading off of it. We did not like it at all, but it was a start. We needed a few pieces of furniture and got ripped off by a few unscrupulous people who took advantage of us.

June - New Zealand

It was a shaky start but June and I could see the potential of where we were. It was good but we would have to work to improve our lot. I became a little despondent at that time but June remained steadfast despite these difficulties.

We found a nice house but lost it after putting in our offer. We were very disappointed with our loss as the house would have been ideal for us with plenty of room. We referred to it as 'The Green House'.

However, we continued in our search, viewed many houses and eventually stumbled on our ideal home. We found and bought a lovely old sprawling wooden house on a quarter acre, on a hill overlooking the Taieri plain, with the Mungatua Hills a distant view from our large picture window. Better by far than the green house. Our limited financial assets were able to easily afford that as the prices were much lower than further North and as first-time buyers, we qualified for very good mortgage rates.

It was a lovely place and large enough for our big family, with a carport and a garage which I converted into a 'sleepout', which gave us an extra bedroom. June and the boys pitched in wherever they could as it was a large conversion with sliding doors at the front. It was to be Joe's room but the kids all spent lots of time out there too. It enabled them to escape from me and June. The house had three other bedrooms, a sun lounge, a living room, a kitchen/diner, a bathroom, a laundry room, an extra toilet, a large shed and spacious gardens back and front. We were in heaven.

And did we love that house!

Our lovely New Zealand home

Joe   Carl   Austin   Jenny

June - New Zealand

We took up skiing in the wintertime, which was new to us all with lots of fun and a lot of falls. The ski fields were right there on the South Island so it was just a few hours' drive away from home.

We did a lot of exploring and came across several quite treacherous steep dangerous roads with sheer drops at the side. There was far less danger prevention there. You were expected to look after yourself regarding personal safety. We stayed in some very basic cabins during these times and still get a laugh about staying in 'Bunkhouse no. 9'

During my travels between houses, fixing people's TVs I went to one that was most interesting to me. The wall in the living room was full of guitars and one long-neck banjo.

Once I had repaired the TV I rather cheekily asked if I could try one of the guitars. We talked music, and Christine, the lady of the house showed a lot of interest and asked me to come back later when her husband was home. They had a small band and needed a bass player. Well, how lucky for me.

I joined the group as a bass guitarist playing country music which was very popular in the South Island, but this was interspersed with some Maori songs as our singer, the aforementioned lady of the house, Christine, was Maori. I learned one of those songs myself after getting my head around the Maori words and still do it today on occasion. I loved the way that the Maori culture permeated society. Maori culture was integrated into the society, including in school and there was much respect for their history and traditions. The kids learned Maori songs and were taught about Maori culture.

Travels with an old guitar

It was one of the nice things about New Zealand that Maori and 'Pakeha' (the rest of us ex-Europeans) cultures were intertwined.

Here`s a little story about one of my TV repair jobs.

I was in a Maori house ready to repair their TV and as I went round the back the man said to me, "Hey man, it's still plugged in."

I replied, "Oh! That's ok", whereupon he said something to his kids in Maori and they all burst out laughing.

I said."What did you say to them?"

He replied," I told them we were going to have Pakeha for dinner." after which we all laughed.

After living there for a short while you got quite used to pronouncing words that had at first been real tongue twisters.

. June, Joe, Austin, and Carl at Cardrona Ski field

We were also lucky with our next-door neighbours Tom and Erin. Tom was a great accordion player. He hadn't been playing much before we arrived, but he and I linked up and formed a duo entertaining the folks nearby. Our arrival had given him a new spark and we played some good music together spending many Saturday nights playing tunes and singing songs visiting neighbours with our instruments.

Then I went panning for gold. I developed this interesting new pastime panning for gold in the hills.

Otago, the province where we lived had a gold rush in the past and there was still gold in "them thar hills". The miners would simply move on if they heard of larger strikes elsewhere, but the gold was still there.

My neighbour John used to frequently go into the hills in search of gold and I would go with him, with the permission of the farmers who owned the land. Another friend who came with us had made a 'cradle', which is a device that the prospectors used as a means of processing more sediment. We would go to likely places where there might be gold and dig in the streambed.

The cradle was a wooden box contraption rather like a baby's cradle with a handle for rocking. Inside were a series of slats that we covered with sackcloth. One of us would shovel the sediment into the top, another would pour water in to wash it down, the third would rock the cradle and as the gravel was washed past the slats any gold would get trapped in the sackcloth because of its weight. After doing this for a while, we would carefully remove the sackcloth wash it into a gold pan and pan it in the river. And we did find gold. Not enough to pay off the mortgage, but there it was sparkling in the pan, which was very exciting. We never got rich but it was great fun.

John told me later of another of his exploits. He had been secretly cultivating a crop of marijuana in a remote location up in the hills hidden by surrounding bushes and when he went there he would find lots of stoned rabbits wandering around.

So we adapted to our new Kiwi lives and made the most of it.

June and I loved walking and we found some great places in the hills thereabouts up and down the coast of Otago. The kids all got involved with various clubs and were integrating into their schools well and making friends.

My firm flew me on courses a few times to Auckland where their main centre was, to learn about the latest version of VCRs.

June secured a job in a local child nursery and was happy working there. She also took courses in psychology. She, like me, had had a limited education and had gone straight into Nursery Nursing at a young age.

When Christmas came it was mid-summer which was a little strange to us, but we took advantage of it and took a trip all around the South Island. Nelson and the beaches at Tahunanui at the top end of the South Island was one of my favourite places and I wrote a song about it sometime later.

Matukituki Glacier

From Nelson we drove down the West Coast to visit defunct gold mines, and on to Te Anau in the far South where we were devoured by mosquitos. There were millions of them and all you could do was run for cover. My work colleagues told me that they like Pommy's blood.

One of the social differences that we found while living in New Zealand was that it was a man's world. Women and girls had a harder time of it in some ways than boys as June and Jenny discovered.

June wanted to open a bank account and needed my permission! How crazy was that? Jenny told us that if a question was asked in school they would never ask the girls, just the boys. The girls were being trained to be good housewives and she had just come from lively old England where things were far more modern and exciting for a young girl. She hated the place, although she did develop some very good girlfriends that she still keeps in touch with.

Apart from our little tribe, two other Pommy families were working at my firm and they seemed keen to create a Pommy club. I didn't like that at all. I knew well from experience that the only way to be a successful immigrant was to integrate. The other two guys wanted us three and our wives to meet up frequently and be separate from the locals. I had no liking for the idea. They were people that I would normally have nothing to do with. One of the guys just wanted to have booze-ups every weekend. The other guy was a crook. I liked the Kiwis and I liked the culture, the weather, and the easy-going way of life suited me well.

Carl and Austin's dad, Andy came out from England to visit us and that coincided with my brother Ronn and his wife Daphne coming from Australia too so we had a large house full.

Travels with an old guitar

Mohammer Country Music Festival near Oamaru,
South Island, N.Z. 1988 ish

New Zealand is a wonderful place and June and I loved it. We
assimilated into the country completely. I loved the prevailing
attitude there which was easy-going, friendly, and happy. The
climate was good with longer summers than we were used to
and for the first time in my life I enjoyed wintertime, as
although it could get cold, the skies were often blue and it
would generally warm up in the daytime, and we would ski
whenever we could.

I was happy. I had a good job travelling around the Taieri
Plain repairing people's TVs and meeting many friendly
people who would give me home-grown vegetables, and a
coffee, and even offer me dinner sometimes. We had a lovely

home. People had welcomed us and we had integrated into the Kiwi life well.

I had been caught once in my life by not taking out citizenship in Canada when I should have done, and I was not going to be caught twice, so I insisted that we all become New Zealand citizens.

New Zealand had been great for us, we had had a great life there but after about five years changes came once more.

When she had finished her schooling Jenny wanted to go back to Canada to see her mum and although she had a few hiccups at first, she liked the place enough to stay. She continued with some further education there.

Carl went back to England to join the Parachute Regiment, which was his dream. He was always very interested in the military.

Joe took an apprenticeship in electronics, the same trade as me repairing TVs and Video Recorders. He had moved out and was house-sharing with some buddies from school

So it was down to just June, Austin and me.

Carl was only fifteen when he went back to England and June was concerned about his welfare, so after a few months she decided that she would like to return too to make sure that he was okay, and also to visit her aged parents again.

I have to admit that I also had a hankering to see Canada again, the place where I had effectively grown up and had so many adventures. Canada was still in my blood. So I was somewhat conflicted in my desires. I loved both New Zealand and Canada. My spirit of wandering was still there.

So at that point, I agreed with June to go back temporarily to England with her and Austin.

Austin   Carl   Jenny   Joe

After a few years, Joe too decided to go to see his birthplace of Canada, where he also made a new life for himself.

So our lives consequently moved on from New Zealand but as I write, it looks as if our citizenship there is going to benefit the next generation. Two of Carl's children, now have New Zealand passports, a great asset for young people in today's world of restricted travel.

In my many travels through life, I have left behind me some wonderful places. In retrospect, as we look back, June and I agreed that New Zealand would have been a great place to settle down.

Selling our lovely home nearly broke my heart

* * *

27

CONCLUSIONS

All of the foregoing events are now disappearing into the mists of the past for me, great memories though they are. There is a little more to come so here is an outline of where we all went from there.

All of our children are either married or coupled. Their multi-national childhood gave them all a great world experience which cannot be such a bad thing and they are all happy and settled in their lives. Joe, Carl, Jenny and Austin all have talents in different areas and they all get together whenever they are not scattered far and wide. They shared much of their early lives in England and New Zealand and still share a great bond.

Jenny took up acting for a while back in Canada. She even starred in a small production film. She joined the White Rock Players, the theatrical group that her grandfather Reg had been in when she was a baby. Sadly he had died in the intervening years but she did get to meet and join some of those people who were his good friends in the acting world and acted with them herself. It would have been so good had she been able to go back in time to join him on the stage. It would have been just wonderful for both of them.

Her partner Richard has a recording studio in Vancouver and every time I have visited I have made a recording that he has very professionally mastered. He was a professional musician himself but now prefers running his recording studio. So I now have about a dozen first-class recordings, on some of which I have Jenny singing backing vocals. Quite enough to make an album.

Jenny is a trained counsellor and has worked in that field for many years, but after doing a Master's degree in creative writing in Wales has now become a writer. She always wrote the most interesting letters and had a great talent with words.

She also recently took a course in teaching and because of her background in counselling, she now teaches that subject at University.

Joe worked as an electronics engineer for a few years and now has a good job with a wiring and computerised alarm systems company and is doing very well in central B.C. with his partner Sheri. They also have a holiday retreat high in the mountains with the bears. We try to visit each other as often as we can.

Joe   Jim   Jenny

Austin served several years in the army and now runs his own business in the house maintenance field and is also doing well. He is married to a lovely girl named Leanne and has two boys. They have a very happy life together in their home near Southampton

And so life goes on to the next generation.

After serving in the Paras Carl has worked in senior management in the security business in London. He is married and has produced three children, a boy and two girls, the oldest of whom, Luke, I had the greatest pleasure in being granddad to and spending lots of time with when he was small. We had heaps of fun together and I got to fully appreciate what a wonderful thing it is to be a granddad.

Travels with an old guitar

Jim and Luke

For all of my life, I have written poems as life happened to me, often about the humorous things that you might observe in life, and sometimes of a more romantic theme, but being a granddad certainly gave the inspiration for one of those moments. Being a granddad was wonderful.
So here it is......

Conclusions

BEING GRANDDAD...

It's a marvellous thing being granddad,
To a person so tiny and new.
How amazing to hold such a treasure.
All bundled in pink, or blue.

What a wonderful thing to be granddad
To a boy with eyes bright and wide
As you tell him the tale of the monster
While under the covers he'll hide.

There's nothing like being granddad
To a boy who pulls worms from the ground
As you sprawl on the grass to watch insects
And share in the treasures he's found.

And what it is to be somebody's granddad
To a girl with pink dresses and curls
To be placed in the front row to watch her
As she dances and curtsies and twirls.

And it's something to be her best granddad
As you sip her imaginary tea.
And cherish the cake that she made you
Quite the best, you're pretending to see.

Travels with an old guitar

There's nothing that beats being granddad
Or the reach from a tiny hand.....
It's riches to count beyond measure
More than all the wealth in the land.

My brother Ronn went to live in Perth, Western Australia with his wife Daphne, and they have had a wonderful life there with their three children and now grandchildren.

My brother Paul, sensibly, remained in Canada and has also had a good life there. He has a daughter from his previous marriage and he and his wife Jackie have three daughters, and they too have grandchildren.

Paul employed our cousin, Brendan, in his business as a favour, but he began stealing the products and selling them privately. He had no regrets at all when Paul confronted him. He was built with a different set of values from us and we have long since lost contact. Last time I saw him he was making his living in a very dubious trade.

Coming back to England made it a full circle for me. After wandering around the world I had come back to where it all started.

My ageing mum could no longer manage her affairs on her own so she was glad to have me around to help. She had nobody else and that is a part of the reason that I am still here in England. We had some very good times and much laughter together. I would visit her frequently in Brighton by train for the last few years of her life.

Conclusions

She had been a great mum and had been there for me when I needed help in the past. Her body was old and frail. Her hearing and sight were going but her mind was fully intact, and she could still beat us all in a game of Scrabble. If there was a dispute over a word if she hadn't heard of it it didn't exist. I'm glad to say she never lost her sense of humour.

I had spent all of my youth growing up in Brighton and the town was full of nostalgia for me. I have frequently ambled through the lanes, and down to the seafront where I had wandered so many times as a boy. I would amble along the seashore and gaze out at the skeletal remains of the West Pier, now just a barren island of rusting girders just offshore, and I remember how one warm summer day my dad, my brothers and I had swum around it when it was still a thriving concern. When Dad proposed this I said, "Dad, I don't think I can do this."

"Yes you can," he said, so off we went.

We had to give a very wide berth as we got to the end of the pier because of the fishermen, so it made for a very long swim, but we all managed it ok. I can still remember the worst part, swimming back under the dark pier between the girders, wondering what creatures lurked below. I wrote a poem with this place in mind about a creature who lived there called 'The Great Purple Ludicrus'

All things must pass.

I always loved Brighton and I still do. It remains a unique place of great character full of interesting people and places. Jenny often comes with me and she also feels a great affinity with the town. We often see my old buddy Sir Peter and his wife Lady Margaret and on occasion stay overnight with them.

My mum outlived all of her siblings by a long way and reached the grand age of ninety-five, just like her mother. I would love to be able to spend just one more day with her listening to those fascinating stories about her childhood as a young girl growing up in a poor household in Brighton in the 1920s and 30s. She still had a great memory of those times and could tell a good story. She even wrote a book about herself, recounting her childhood and what it was like to grow up in Brighton in those far-off days. I also remember sitting at the feet of her mother, my grandmother, and hearing her tales of Brighton in the Victorian age. It gave me a direct connection to that history of so long ago.

My dad died in the year 2000 at the age of seventy-nine. He was just a couple of weeks short of his eightieth birthday but he had an early eightieth birthday party celebration anyway at my house, as my brother Paul and his family were in England on holiday. Dad's end was perfectly fitting for him as he had just given a sermon and died as he stepped out of the pulpit. It was a good ending for him in the right place.

Conclusions

Auntie Grace in Lymington

I have come and gone from Canada many times since then and kept up my long-standing friendships with my old pals there. We go back a very long way now to those far-off psychedelic times.

June and I had a great life together bringing up four children in New Zealand where we had some fabulous times, but as a part of this conclusion, I have to add that we eventually parted ways amicably after being back in England for a few years. I must be lucky at cards.

We just drifted apart. There was no other reason. June sought a new life and now lives in Sussex where it all started for us, but we are still very good friends and see each other and speak on the phone often and have been a great support to each other through various trials. We have a lot of history together and still have happy family gatherings when Joe or Jenny is over from Canada.

So that covers what happened to everybody mentioned in my family.

Well, that brings us almost to the end of my story, but not quite. There is just one more tale to tell.

28

MOMENTS IN PARADISE

A few years ago I was at home fiddling with something or other while my TV was on in the background. I was not paying much attention to it, and the show 'This Is Your Life' was playing. The subject of the show that week was the English D.J. Dave Lee Travis, and right at the end of the show the host announced,

"...And now, flown in, especially for you all the way from Canada, your old pal Keith Hampshire." This grabbed my attention immediately. It was also my old pal Keith from my band in Calgary. Keith had spent time in England after the band had gone our different ways and had done well there as a DJ on Radio Caroline, the pirate ship. Hence he was a pal of D.L.T. as he is known, and all the other DJs of that era.

I had lost touch with Keith years ago, so I wrote to the TV production company and they put us back in touch with one another. He was as surprised to make contact again as I was. We communicated by email and had a lot of catching up to do. We were able to remind each other of things that we had long since forgotten. He had no recollection of our trip to Saskatoon together, and he reminded me of things I could not recollect at all, like our playing with Roy Orbison. After his episode as a

Travels with an old guitar

DJ on the Pirate ship, Keith had returned to Canada, raised horses in Ontario; had a couple of number-one hits there, and built himself quite a reputation. He still did some D/J work and with his big voice did a lot of voice-over ads on radio and TV. He had a website and was therefore easy to locate for anyone who looked.

And that brings me back to Gayle.

About a year after Keith and I had re-connected, he forwarded an email to me that he had received. It read,

"Hi, Keith. Do you remember me? I am Gayle and I used to go out with Jimmy Brown. Do you know what happened to him?"

My heart went into overdrive. I could not believe it. To put it mildly, I was excited. I replied straightway to Gayle, and she was as pleased to hear from me as I was to hear from her.

And so ensued a rapid interchange of emails between us. They were cautious at first, not giving too much away, but soon became a white heat of re-kindled passion. It had been the first love for both of us all those years ago. She was at the end of her marriage and although I was still on the best of terms with June, we were divorced and I was single and free, so the sparks flew between us. She was still in Calgary but also had a house in Palm Springs California, and after a few weeks of writing, and talking on the phone, with the flames burning ever higher, she told me that she was going down there to stay for a while and said,

"Would you like to come?"

Do I need to tell you my reply?

262

So one day in September I boarded a plane from Gatwick to Calgary. I was so nervous. Gayle was so nervous. This was a special moment for us so she hired a photographer for the occasion and we have the photos of our long-delayed meeting, after not seeing each other for 42 years.

I emerged from the baggage hall and there was my beautiful Gayle running toward me. It was a moment for us both that words can barely describe.

And so began one of the most amazing, incredible times that I have had in all of my life. She had booked a hotel room for that night in Calgary, and the following morning we set off in her lovely sports car, heading South for the border.

The conversation with the USA customs official was quite amusing.

Moments in Paradise

'How long have you known each other?' We were an unlikely couple after all as I lived in England and Gayle in Canada. We replied "Over 40 years". But in the end, the border guard lady who was asking us these questions had to smile.

This was another one of those moments for me for poetic inspiration...

A MOMENT IN TIME

The Fifth of September was a day of great joy
For a girl from the West and a wandering boy.
A moment in time when treasures were found
There, 'midst the noise, hearing never a sound.
But their thundering hearts scarcely contained.
Control, composure, barely maintained.
At an airport for a long-delayed rendezvous
And a joining that somehow was way overdue.
With eyes unmet more than forty long years
Unfocussed now with uncontrolled tears.
Now she runs to his arms as they rush to embrace
A moment that nothing can ever replace.
All the world passes by, and glances are cast
But all is unseen as each is held fast.
A moment in time that belonged to just two,
Forever remembered. Just me. Just you.

(for Gayle)
(I was always a romantic at heart)

Travels with an old guitar

While I was there in Calgary I had also arranged to meet Terry, my old guitar-playing buddy, from the band. We met in the lobby of the hotel and had trouble recognising each other after all those years, but we did and it was just great to see him again. Terry had gone on to have an interesting career himself playing in bands backing some famous, and as he said, some 'would be' famous people and touring through the USA.

Terry and Jim

So back to Gayle and our great reunion. We drove down through Montana, Utah, and Arizona, where I saw real tumbleweeds for the first time, taking me back to those old cowboy movies that I had been raised on, and from there we drove on into Nevada, staying in various motels on the way.

When we got to Las Vegas and told the desk clerk of our situation he gave us a honeymoon suite, which was just fabulous, high up in the building with a terrific view. Jenny and Richard flew down from Vancouver to meet us and we had a few wonderful days there enjoying the food, the sun, the swimming pool, the atmosphere, and more than anything else, each other.

Las Vegas was a first for me.

After staying there for a few days we drove on to Gayle's house in Palm Springs California where she showed us some of the local sights, such as Frank Sinatra's house, Dean Martin Drive, Bob Hope's mansion on top of the hill, and all the rest. She had a lovely house with lemons growing in her garden which was a novel thing for me, and there were hummingbirds that I had never seen before. It was all just wonderful and I was a very, very happy man.

After staying there for a few days, we drove on to Disneyland in Anaheim, booked a couple of motel rooms for the four of us and immersed ourselves in the Magic Kingdom. It was Jenny and Richard's favourite place. They had been there many times but I had not been for a very long time. The whole experience had been like a dream for me. I had been transported to paradise.

Moments in Paradise

Disneyland

Travels with an old guitar

But then the time came that I had to leave. I was still working so had had to limit my stay to about three weeks. Jenny and Richard had flown back to Vancouver by then so the parting between me and Gayle came again, but we had re-kindled a great fire.

I returned to my home in England and my job, but I had a new light in my life. Some months later, Gayle flew over to join me in England and she lived here with me for about six months, which was the maximum time that she was allowed to remain in England. She met my musical friends and we had a ball.

Gayle is a great piano player and sometimes we would come across a piano in the pub where we were playing music so she was a great addition to the music. We bought a couple of ukuleles and had fun with those too as we travelled along. It was so good to share songs and to sing harmonies, and more than that, just to share our love of music and to be together.

It was during this time while Gayle was with me in England that Keith came over with his wife Cathy and stayed with us. It was a great reunion for us and we had so much catching up to do as we talked of old times.

Keith was still living in Ontario doing those voice-over jobs in the media. While he was with me I was able to give him some copies of the old studio photos that I had of the band back in Calgary which he then put up on his website. Keith and Cathy also had children and grandchildren.

Keith   Cathy   Gayle   Jim

Some months after she had gone back home, Gayle was back in Calgary and I flew over once more to join her. This time it happened to be Stampede week again so it was another nostalgic trip for me as we wandered around the stampede grounds together. It had been over forty years since I had been there on my hitchhiking trip with my brother Paul.

We stayed with Gayle's mum who remembered me. It was good to see her again after all those years, and it was lovely to wander around Calgary again with Gayle.

Back to Cowboy town

We drove from there to visit her two daughters, Justine and Shannon in Medicine Hat and stayed with them there for a few days. Medicine Hat was the place where I had abandoned the train to hitchhike to Calgary all those years before. I had trouble recognising anyplace though.

After Medicine Hat, we went West back to Calgary and after a short visit there we took a long drive, stopping here and there, through the Rockies, Central B.C., and eventually on to Vancouver where we met up with Jenny and Joe and some of my old pals. While we were there we made another recording at Richard's studio, this time with Gayle singing backing vocals and harmonies.

Once again I had to fly back home but Gayle returned to England again to join me for another few months. Our time was always limited because of restrictions on visitors to the UK, and my need to look after my mum.

And that brings me to almost the end of my story. Life goes on for us all and I'm sure there is a lot more to write about on this journey through our fascinating world but I will tie it all together here with just a few final conclusions.

29

LYMINGTON

Gayle and I had some of the best times of our lives together. We were playing in the same key and shared the very happiest of times, and it would be perfect to end this story with our wonderful reunion. The story would be complete. How lovely it would be to end there.

But life is a convoluted journey.

We had obstacles to overcome on many levels, not least geographical. We shared many similar views on the joys of life and lived them to the full but some things came between us that were hard to overcome.

I had to remain in England because of commitments here and Gayle's home and heart were in the USA.

We also had a divergence of opinion on some of the larger issues. She was deeply involved with a political group whose philosophy was a world away from my own and this unfortunately impinged greatly on our relationship.

In the end, sad to say, these things got in the way of what might have been.

Gayle and I shared an amazing, incredible chapter in our

lives which we both treasure, but a life together was not to be.

I am still here in England, in Lymington, and Gayle is in California but we won't forget those amazing times that we shared together.

So although many miles separate us now, Gayle has played a big part in my life story ever since that day way back in 1964 when I walked in with the band and she set her eyes upon me.

Travels with an old guitar

So life goes on and going forward a few years, the next thing that happened to me is that I fell under a train. Yes, I fell under a train. Yet another experience in my varied life.

I was returning from a trip to Canada and heading home when disaster struck.

I was at Brighton station with just two minutes left before my train departed and was running along the platform when I passed out.

The next thing I knew when I came around was that I was in that very small gap between the train and the platform, lying on my backpack. On one side of me was the huge train wheel, on the other, the wall of the platform.

I knew immediately where I was and said to myself,

"Oh-------". Well, use your imagination. I tried climbing out but a man who must have seen me roll off the platform was leaning over and told me to stay put as an ambulance was on its way. They turned the power off of the rail and the paramedics, with some difficulty, stretchered me out of that small gap and took me to the hospital. I had managed to stop all the trains which must have upset a lot of people.

I had fallen flat on my face on the platform before passing out breaking many bones. The doctors were going to repair me but after many tests, they concluded that the reason I had passed out was that my heart was in serious trouble. So instead they gave me an open heart operation where they replaced my faulty aortic valve. My facial bones were left to self-repair. Life was never simple.

Lymington

June has always been a great support for me through many trials and a truly great companion and friend and I must give her credit for always looking out for my welfare. So she came to Brighton to check on me, only for her car to be hit by lightning, whereupon the electrics were demolished, so she never got there. Her car was a write-off.

It was a very eventful day.

That was over five years ago now and I am pleased to say that after several annual checks, my heart is still working fine.

So that brings me right up to the present day as I sit here tapping out my memories.

The writing of all of this and trawling through those memories to retrieve what I can remember of it through my youth and beyond has been a great journey for me. It has amused me and entertained me in re-living those times now long gone and recalling those places that I wandered through on my journey. Memories of the people I met, and the many happy times I had on that long road with my guitar learning about life and singing a few songs along the way has been a fascinating trip. I never did meet up with those Hula girls but I had a grand old time anyway.

We only get this one life and I am so glad that I did the things that I did.

When I invent a time machine I'm going to go back to do it all again.

Travels with an old guitar

Jim Brown

Special thanks to Monica Fulford for her patience in going through the earlier texts for me and offering me her good advice

.

And to my daughter Jenny Brown
for her great input and suggestions on edits

* * *

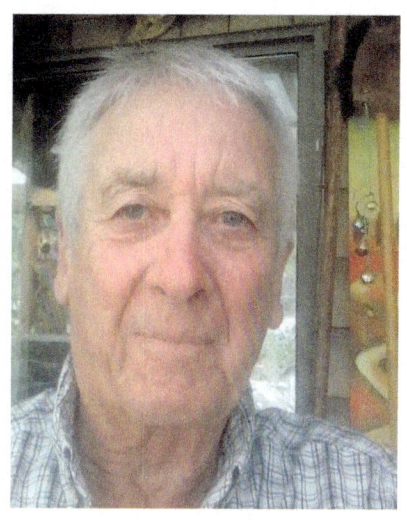

Jim Brown was born in Brighton, Sussex in 1946. He is currently compiling a book of his poems entitled 'Poems of Laughter, Love, and Lament'

He has played music since he was a teenager and has played bass guitar in bands in England, Canada and New Zealand. He still plays guitar and banjo and sings regularly in pubs with friends.

He now lives in Lymington, Hampshire in the New Forest, England.

Printed in Great Britain
by Amazon